THE HUNTING & FISHING LIBRARY®

FISHING MAN-MADE LAKES

By Dick Sternberg

DICK STERNBERG grew up fishing small reservoirs in southern Minnesota, and has fished practically every type of man-made lake in North America, from swampland reservoirs in Louisiana to Canadian Shield reservoirs in the wilds of Canada.

CY DECOSSE INCORPORATED
Chairman: Cy DeCosse
President: James B. Maus
Executive Vice President: William B. Jones

FISHING MAN-MADE LAKES
Author and Project Director: Dick Sternberg
Editor: Janice Cauley
Project Managers: John van Vliet, Joseph Cella
Senior Art Director: Bradley Springer
Research and Photo Director: Eric Lindberg
Researchers: Steven Hauge, Mike Hehner, Jim Moynagh
Principal Photographers: Mike Hehner, William Lindner
Photo Assistants: Steven Hauge, Jim Moynagh
Staff Photographer: John Lauenstein
Director of Development Planning and Production: Jim Bindas
Production Manager: Amelia Merz
Electronic Publishing Specialist: Joe Fahey
Production Staff: Diane Dreon-Krattiger, Mike Schauer, Dave Schelitzche, Nik Wogstad
Illustrators: Thomas Boll, Mike Zirbes, Brad Springer
Contributing Photographers: Joseph Anselmi; Frank Balthis; Howard Beckstrom/Tony Stone Worldwide Ltd.; Dick Cassidy, Joseph Tanner/ U.S. Army Corps of Engineers; Jed Dekalb/Tennessee State Photo Services; Russ Finley; Steven Hauge; Iowa Soil Conservation Service; Johnstown Area Heritage Association; Dennis Kleve; Chuck Meyer/ U.S. Department of the Interior; Cliff Redmon; Bradley Springer; U.S. Bureau of Reclamation; John van Vliet; Don Wirth

Primary Reservoir Limnology Advisor: Kent Thornton, FTN Associates Ltd.

Cooperating Individuals and Agencies: Bureau of Reclamation, Rio Grande Project – Dan Page; Conley Bottom Resort – Van Back; Dakota Limit Guide Service – Rod Irion; Dinosaurland Travel Board – Marion Eason; Jim Elmore; Federal Emergency Management Agency – William S. Bivins; Flaming Gorge Corp. – Jerry Taylor; Florida Game and Fish Commission – Tom Champeau; Ronnie Grant; Grider Hill Dock – Tony Sloan; Indiana Department of Natural Resources – Robert Ball; Iowa Department of Natural Resources – Marion Conover; Jim's Bait Service – Jim Keuten; Johnstown Area Heritage Association – Dan Ingram;

Kentucky Department of Fish and Wildlife Resources – David Bell, Doug Stephens ; Lee Klaprodt; Ko-no-ko Guide Service – Joe Walleen, Jr.; Lake of the Woods Control Board – Rick Cousins; Louisiana Department of Culture, Recreation, and Tourism – Wylie Harvey; Louisiana Department of Wildlife and Fisheries – Charles Hoenke; Marina Tackle Store – Rodger McKown; Minnesota Department of Natural Resources – Ed Feiler; Minnesota Geological Survey – G. B. Morey; Nebraska Game and Parks Commission – Joel Klammer; New Mexico Department of Game and Fish – Ernie Jaquez, Jack Kelley; New Mexico Environment Department – David Tague; New Mexico Water Resources Research Institute, New Mexico State University – Tom Bahr; New Town Chamber of Commerce – Jeff Gronos; Morris Nielsen; North Dakota Game and Fish Department – Greg Power, Tom Pruitt, Terry Steinwand; North Dakota Parks and Tourism – Jim Fuglie; Ontario Ministry of Natural Resources – Paul McMahon; Ontario Ministry of Tourism and Recreation – Mike Furlong; Spenser Owens; Peabody Coal Company – Joyce Fitzgerald; Billy Ray; Rodger's Guide Service – Rodger Affeldt; Mike Settle; Tarrant Co. Water District – Mike Williams; Tennessee Valley Authority – Larry Richardson, Rick Woodlee; Texas Parks and Wildlife Department – Ken Kerkowski, Richard Ott, Kevin Storei; Jim Thill; Truth or Consequences Chamber of Commerce – Marilyn Pittsenbarger; U.S. Army Corps of Engineers – John Ferrell, Paul Johnston, Sam Powell, Craig Shoe; Utah Department of Natural Resources – Steve Brayton; Wyoming Fish and Game Department – Bill Wengert

Contributing Manufacturers: Abu-Garcia Inc.; A.C. Shiners, Inc.; Alumacraft Boat Co.; Bagley Bait Co.; Banks, Inc.; Berkley, Inc.; Bill Lewis Lures; Blue Fox Tackle Co.; Bobbie Bait Co.; Bomber Bait Co.; Bullet Weights, Inc.; Bulldog Lures, Inc.; Cannon/S&K Products, Inc.; Canyon Lures, Inc.; Classic Mfg./Culprit Lures, Inc.; The Coleman Company; D & K Distributors; Daiwa Corp.; Ditto Products; Drifter Bait Co.; Eppinger Mfg. Co.; Feldmann Eng. & Mfg. Co., Inc.; Fenwick; GNB Incorporated/Stowaway Batteries; G. J. and H. Company; Gooch Tackle Co.; Harrison-Hoge Industries, Inc.; Hart Tackle Co., Inc.; Hopkins Fishing Lures Co., Inc.; Joe Bucher Tackle Co.; Johnson Fishing Inc.; Lindy-Little Joe, Inc.; Lowrance Electronics, Inc.; Luck "E" Strike, USA; Luhr-Jensen & Sons; Lund Boats; Lunker City; Mann's Bait Co.; Mar-Lyn Lure Co.; Mercury Marine-Mariner Outboards; Mister Twister, Inc.; O. Mustad & Son; Normark Corp.; Northland Fishing Tackle; Owner American Corp.; Plano Molding Company; Poe's Lure Co.; Pradco; Professional Sporting Goods; Q&S Mfg./ Wille Products, Inc.; St. Croix Rods; Si-Tex Marine Electronics, Inc.; Slater's Jigs; Smithwick Lures Inc.; Stanley Jigs, Inc.; Storm Mfg., Inc.; Suick Lure Manufacturers; Sylo's Inc./Divin' Ace; Tru-Turn Inc.; Uncle Josh Bait Co.; Wazp Brand Products; Weedless Lures, Inc.; Windel's Tackle Co.; Yakima Bait Co.; Zak Tackle Manufacturing; Zebco Corp.

Printing: R. R. Donnelley & Sons, Co. (0193)

Library of Congress
Cataloging-in-Publication Data
Sternberg, Dick.
Fishing Man-made Lakes / by Dick Sternberg.
p. cm. – (The Hunting & fishing library)
Includes index.
ISBN 0-86573-040-7 (hardcover)
1. Fishing–United States. 2. Reservoirs–United States–Recreational use.
I. Title. II. Series.
SH463.P734 1993   92-32566
799.1'1 – dc20

Contents

Introduction

Man-made lakes have dramatically altered the fishing habits of millions of North American anglers. Small-stream fishermen have been converted to big-lake fishermen, and a whole new fishing-oriented economy has developed around hundreds of major reservoirs.

And, as every convert knows, the transition from stream fishing to reservoir fishing is not easy – nor is switching from natural-lake to reservoir fishing. First, there are many different kinds of fish. Second, even the original species behave differently after a river or stream is impounded.

Thousands of books have been written on fishing in natural lakes, rivers and streams, but very few books focus solely on man-made lakes. The purpose of this book is to acquaint you with the most important kinds of man-made lakes, and show you exactly where to find and how to catch every major gamefish species in each of these waters.

The first section, "Understanding Man-made Lakes," explains why reservoirs are built, how they work, and how they differ from natural lakes in terms of water temperature and clarity, oxygen content, water-level fluctuations and many other factors that affect your angling strategy. You'll also learn about various types of dams and how different parts of a dam function.

The second section, "Fishing Man-made Lakes," features seven separate case studies, each focusing on an important reservoir type. An individual case study highlights a specific man-made lake, but is representative of many other lakes of the same type. So even if you never have the opportunity to fish any of our featured reservoirs, the information will help you catch fish in any similar lake.

Each case study will help you understand how that particular type of man-made lake differs from other important types. A desert reservoir, for instance, has considerably different fish habitat than a swampland reservoir, and undergoes much greater water-level fluctuation. Consequently, strategies for finding fish and following them throughout the year are completely different.

Angling techniques also differ greatly from one reservoir to another. This book demonstrates the methods that work best for each important species of gamefish in each type of lake, including the right tackle, lures and bait.

Keep in mind that techniques shown in one case study may also work in other types of waters. Many of the methods we've included are the favorites of prominent guides and tournament fishermen who specialize in fishing a specific type of reservoir, but their tactics will work equally well in many other lakes, man-made or otherwise.

So don't be afraid to try a new approach on your favorite lake – you might just find that the fish will welcome the change.

Understanding Man-made Lakes

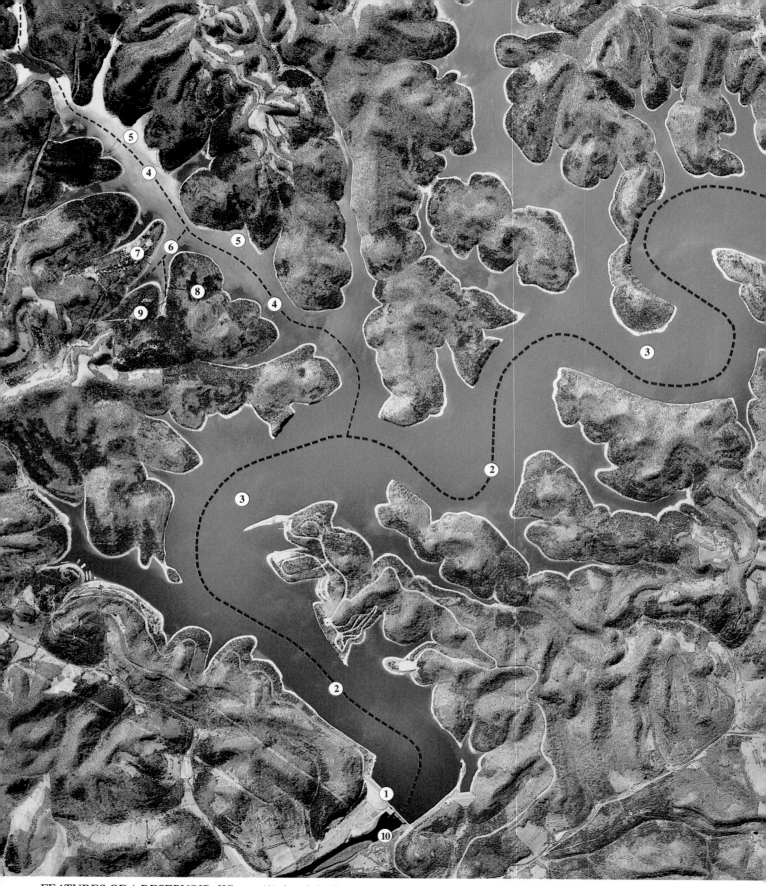

FEATURES OF A RESERVOIR. When a (1) dam is built, the (2) main river channel is flooded, forming the (3) main lake. Where major creeks flowed into the river, (4) main creek channels are flooded, forming (5) main creek arms. The main creeks may be joined by smaller, or *secondary*, creeks. When (6) secondary creek channels are flooded, (7) secondary creek arms form. Smaller, or *tertiary* creeks may enter secondary creeks. When (8)

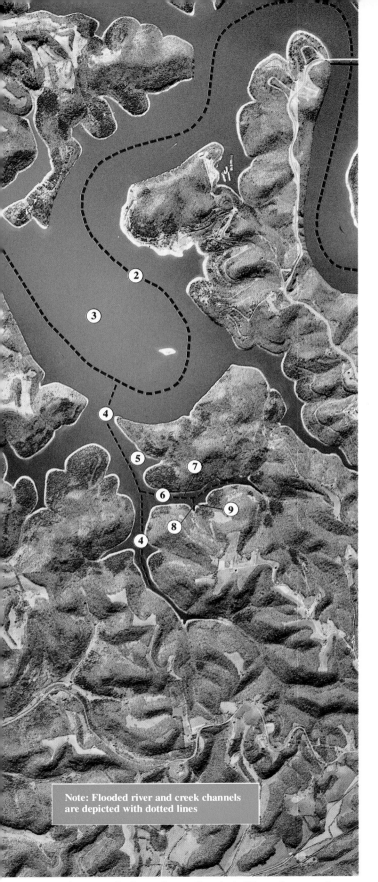

Note: Flooded river and creek channels are depicted with dotted lines

Reservoir Basics

Historians believe that the first dam was constructed in ancient Egypt around 2800 B.C., for the main purpose of creating a permanent supply of drinking water. North America's first dams were most likely built around 800 A.D., by Arizona's Hohokam Indians, to supply water for irrigation and drinking. By the year 1900, only about 100 major dams existed in the United States.

The dam-building era really began in the 1930s, with creation of the Tennessee Valley Authority (TVA) in 1933 and passage of the Flood Control Act of 1936. By 1990, more than 80,000 reservoirs of 500 acres or more had been constructed in the United States alone.

The Bureau of Reclamation, the U.S. Army Corps of Engineers and the TVA have built the majority of large reservoirs in this country, but many have also been constructed by power companies and local units of government. Construction costs vary from several million dollars for a small dam to more than a billion for a large one, such as Arizona's Glen Canyon Dam, which impounds Lake Powell.

Some reservoirs are still being built, but with more and more of the prime dam sites already developed, the rate of increase in reservoir acreage has diminished greatly.

Practically all government reservoirs are built to solve water-related problems. But reservoirs may also create new problems. Sometimes projects are delayed for years while various special-interest groups argue their cases in court.

Regardless of the reasons for proposing construction of a reservoir, the overall benefits must outweigh the

tertiary creek channels are flooded, (9) tertiary creek arms form. After the reservoir fills, the flooded channels are called the "old" river or creek channels. The river immediately below the dam is the (10) tailwaters.

EFFECTS of reservoir construction are demonstrated by these before, during and after photographs. The top photo shows the river and eventual reservoir basin before the dam was built; notice the forested area along the river corridor. In the middle photo, the dam has been constructed, and the river corridor cleared of timber. The bottom photo shows the reservoir after it has filled.

drawbacks for the project to proceed. Following are the most common reasons for building reservoirs:

FLOOD CONTROL. Most Corps of Engineers dams have been built for this purpose, along with navigation (below). The reservoir is drawn down in late fall, sometimes by 50 feet or more. Then, should spring runoff be heavy, the water simply fills the reservoir rather than flooding communities along the river.

MUNICIPAL WATER SUPPLY. Cities often dam nearby rivers to guarantee a reliable water supply. If water were tapped directly from the river, supplies could fall short when the river is low. On some water-supply lakes, however, outboards are banned, and on others, no fishing is permitted at all.

IRRIGATION. In the desert Southwest and other arid regions, agriculture would be impossible without reservoirs. Streams often dry up completely in summer, just when the need for water to irrigate crops is greatest. The water level in these reservoirs fluctuates greatly from year to year, depending on the amount of runoff.

HYDROELECTRIC POWER. Private utility companies and government agencies, such as the Tennessee Valley Authority, commonly build dams to store water for power generation. The discharge turns turbines to generate economical electric power. Often, the discharge is regulated to correspond to the times of peak power demand.

NAVIGATION. Corps of Engineers dams are often regulated to supply water to downstream rivers during low-water periods. Otherwise, water levels in the rivers would fall too low for passage of towboats and other large vessels. The lower Missouri River, for instance, can accommodate barge traffic most of the year, thanks to water received from reservoirs in the Dakotas.

Irrigation systems get their water from reservoirs, making farming possible in arid regions

Hydroelectric power is produced when reservoir water passes through the turbines in a powerhouse

Cooling lakes stay warm enough year-round to support tropical or marine fish species, such as this redfish

Recreational use is heavy on man-made lakes in densely populated areas

COOLING LAKES. Power companies withdraw large quantities of water from lakes or rivers to cool the steam that drives their turbines. The heated water is sometimes discharged into lakes or ponds, where the temperature drops considerably. Then the water is recirculated or returned to the river.

Anglers enjoy fishing these lakes in winter because the warm discharge causes large numbers of fish to collect in a small area and feed actively.

RECREATION. Regardless of why a reservoir is built, water-based recreation including swimming, boating, scuba diving and fishing is almost always a by-product.

Only in rare cases have large reservoirs been created for the major purpose of recreation. Such lakes are usually located in areas with no other natural or man-made lakes. These waters bolster the local economy by attracting tourists and sometimes by supporting a limited commercial fishery.

North America's Largest Reservoirs (by volume)

RESERVOIR NAME	STATE OR PROVINCE	VOLUME (Thousands of acre ft.)	SURFACE ACRES
Lac Manicougane	Quebec	115,000	511,784
Williston Lake	British Col.	57,006	441,700
Reservoir La Grande #2	Quebec	50,037	700,492
Reservoir La Grande #3	Quebec	48,659	607,620
Lac Caniapiscau	Quebec	43,608	1,058,395
Lake Mead	Ariz. & Nev.	28,537	115,000
Lake Powell	Utah & Ariz.	27,000	108,000
Lake Sakakawea	North Dakota	24,400	368,230
Lake Oahe	N. & S. Dakota	24,288	324,000
Smallwood Reservoir	Newfoundland	22,950	1,408,000
Kinbasket Lake	British Col.	20,000	106,300
Fort Peck Lake	Montana	19,100	212,000
Franklin D. Roosevelt Lake	Washington	9,386	79,400
Lake Diefenbaker	Saskatchewan	8,000	106,210
Kentucky Lake	Ky. & Tenn.	6,129	158,300

How Natural and Man-made Lakes Differ

At first glance, a reservoir and a natural lake of about the same size, shape and fertility would seem identical in most respects. Their water quality and fish populations are similar, but there are more differences than most anglers realize. And many of these differences affect fish location and fishing techniques.

Following are the major ways in which man-made and natural lakes differ:

SHAPE OF BASIN. Dams are usually built across river valleys, so impoundments tend to be long and narrow and the depth increases gradually toward the downstream end. Natural lakes tend to be rounder in shape and the depth often varies greatly throughout the basin.

Man-made lakes generally have three fairly distinct zones, each with different biological and limnological characteristics.

The warm, shallow upper end of the reservoir, where the main river flows in, often has a noticeable current. Because the river carries in sediment, the water is turbid and the basin is partially silted in. Although the water is relatively high in nutrients, the low clarity and current prevent heavy algal blooms. The current usually prevents formation of a thermocline. This zone is best suited to warmwater fish species, although other fish may be present during coolwater periods.

The deeper, cooler lower end includes the pool area above the dam. Because most of the sediment has already settled out, the water is clearer and less fertile than in the upper zone. The lower end most closely resembles a natural lake, with practically no current and a distinct thermocline. If the water is deep and cold enough and has adequate dissolved oxygen, the lower end may support coldwater fish. Warmwater species are often present, but mainly in creek arms and bays rather than in the main lake.

The middle, or transition, area usually has qualities intermediate between the two ends and supports the largest and most varied gamefish crop.

SEDIMENTATION RATE. Because man-made lakes are fed by larger rivers and streams than are natural lakes, sediment accumulates more rapidly. In small reservoirs, the sedimentation rate may approach 2 percent per year, meaning that the reservoir will fill with sediment approximately 50 years after construction. In large reservoirs, the sedimentation rate is usually less than 1 percent per year.

In contrast, the sedimentation rate in most natural lakes ranges from 0.1 to .005 percent per year, meaning a life span of 1000 to 20,000 years.

WATER FERTILITY. Like natural lakes, reservoirs are commonly classified as oligotrophic (infertile), mesotrophic (moderately fertile) or eutrophic (highly fertile) depending upon the amount of nutrients in the water.

The fertility level of natural lakes gradually increases over time. Eventually, all oligotrophic lakes become eutrophic. But in man-made lakes, the eutrophication pattern is different. Normally, fertility peaks within a few years after a reservoir fills, the result of decomposing timber, brush and weeds, and the release of

This reservoir has massive sediment deposits at the upper end (right); little sediment at the lower

nutrients from the soil. These nutrients fuel a fish-production boom (p. 25). Then, the fertility level gradually declines as vegetation disappears and fewer nutrients are leached from the soil, and it remains fairly constant for many years. Nutrient levels will increase, however, in the final stages of the reservoir's life.

In cases where the timber is clear-cut or burned before the reservoir is filled, the boom cycle is comparatively short-lived, because very little vegetation is left to decompose and release nutrients.

The position of a reservoir in relation to other reservoirs on the same river system also affects its fertility level. Upstream reservoirs are "nutrient traps," accumulating nutrients from inflowing streams and preventing them from flowing into downstream reservoirs. Thus, in a series of reservoirs on the same river, the fertility tends to decrease as you move downstream.

Reservoirs with coldwater draws are also less fertile than you might expect. Nutrients that settle into the depths are sometimes discharged almost as rapidly as they accumulate. The lack of fertility means low fish production.

FLUSHING TIME. Also called residence time, this is the amount of time required for natural processes to replace all of the water in a lake. In a natural lake, complete flushing may take hundreds of years. But because man-made lakes receive so much more inflow compared to their volume, the flushing time is much shorter, often less than a year. And in a small reservoir fed by a large river, it could be as little as a day, not enough time for plankton to bloom and start the food chain. This reservoir may not produce as many pounds of fish per acre as a natural lake or a reservoir with a longer flushing time, assuming similar water fertility.

WATER TEMPERATURE. Man-made lakes stratify into temperature layers in much the same way as natural lakes. But there are some important differences. In bottom-draw reservoirs, for instance, the volume of cold water in the depths is reduced over

the course of the summer. As a result, coldwater fish are restricted to a thinner layer of water by summer's end. In a natural lake, the thickness of the coldwater layer decreases more slowly over the summer.

The shallow upstream end of a reservoir is quicker to respond to seasonal air temperature changes than the deeper lower end. For example, the upper end warms faster in spring, not only because the water is shallower, but because the river or stream feeding the reservoir is warmer than the reservoir itself. In fall, the reverse is true, so the upper end cools more rapidly.

OXYGEN CONTENT. Compared to natural lakes, reservoirs are not as likely to experience oxygen levels low enough to cause winterkills. The inflowing water usually furnishes enough oxygen to sustain the fish. But winterkills may occur in eutrophic reservoirs where the inflow is very small compared to the lake's volume. And oxygen levels in eutrophic or mesotrophic reservoirs commonly sag low enough in summer to make the depths off-limits to gamefish.

In some reservoirs, however, cold density currents (below) continually replenish the oxygen supply to the deep water.

DENSITY CURRENTS. Water flowing into a reservoir seeks its own density level. If the inflow is warmer and thus lighter than the surface water in the reservoir, it will form an *overflow,* staying on top of the reservoir water. If the inflow is colder and thus heavier than the coldest water in the reservoir, it will form an *underflow,* hugging the bottom of the reservoir. If the temperature of the inflow is between that at the surface and at the bottom, the water will flow beneath the surface until it reaches the precise depth where the temperature is the same. Then, this *interflow* moves through the reservoir at that depth (diagrams below).

Underflows often result in low fish production. Nutrients carried in by the main river plunge into the depths where they're of little value to fish, because most food organisms live in the shallows. This is a serious problem in some western reservoirs fed by coldwater streams.

Understanding Density Currents   Temperature key: ▢ warm ▢ cool ▢ cold

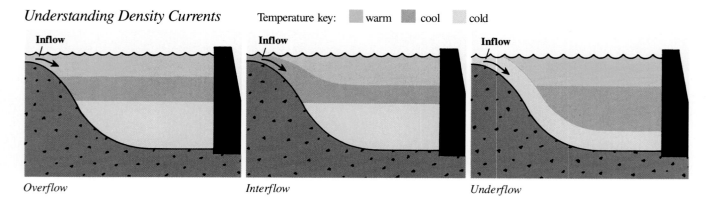

Overflow   Interflow   Underflow

The water is turbid at the upper end (top); clear at the lower

WATER CLARITY. In a natural lake, the water clarity in the main basin tends to be uniform throughout. But in a reservoir, silt carried in by the main river reduces the clarity in the upper reaches. As the water moves downstream, the silt gradually settles out and the clarity increases. The clearest water is immediately above the dam.

WATER-LEVEL FLUCTUATION. The water level in a man-made lake fluctuates much more than in a natural lake. Besides runoff, the main causes of fluctuation are water releases for power generation, flood control, municipal water supply, irrigation and maintaining flow for navigation downstream. Water levels may also be altered to control aquatic vegetation or to better manage fish populations.

Water levels are often kept high during the spawning season. Low water leaves spawning shoals exposed, and there is less flooded vegetation for species that spawn in that type of cover.

AQUATIC VEGETATION. Reservoirs, especially those with widely fluctuating water levels, seldom have the healthy crops of aquatic vegetation so common in natural lakes. When the water drops, the exposed plants dry out and die. During high water, the plants are submerged so far they don't receive adequate sunlight.

Clear-cutting prior to filling a reservoir

As a result, fish in most reservoirs relate more strongly to other types of cover, such as timber, rocks and man-made objects. Most reservoir basins are clear-cut before filling, but sometimes the felled treetops are chained to the remaining stumps to provide cover for fish.

FOOD SUPPLY. Because of greater water-level fluctuations, the supply of fish food in reservoirs is usually not as reliable as in natural lakes.

Most types of baitfish spawn in shallow bays or connecting marshes, so they tend to proliferate at normal to high water stages. When the water is low, their spawning areas are high and dry.

Low water also means reduced inflow of nutrients from feeder streams, and less plankton, the major food for most baitfish. If the water stays low for more than a year, baitfish populations dwindle. And those that remain may be too large for some gamefish to eat. The food scarcity results in decreased gamefish numbers.

Some reservoirs undergo extreme water-level fluctuations

Understanding Dams

Dam design is a complex science. Since the first earthen dam was built nearly 5000 years ago, hundreds of different types of dams have evolved, and that evolution process continues as engineers find better, safer and more economical designs.

Most of the dams that exist today fall into two categories: embankment dams made of natural materials such as rock or compacted earth, and various types of concrete dams. Shown below are examples of the most common kinds of dams.

Types of Embankment Dams

EARTHFILL DAMS. Built mainly from compacted earth, these dams are economical if earthen material is available near the dam site. Sometimes a clay core is required to make the dam watertight. Earthfill dams are usually riprapped to prevent erosion. They are never used in situations where they could be inundated with water.

ROCKFILL DAMS. Often built in mountainous or steep-valleyed terrain where rocky fill is abundant, these dams must have a face of impervious material, such as concrete, or a core of fine earthen materials, to seal them. Earthen-core rockfill dams are the most common type of dam being built today.

ARCH DAMS. These dams are usually built in symmetrical, V-shaped rock canyons with steep sides. Because their shape transfers much of the water's force to the canyon walls, they require less concrete than a gravity dam (below). Arch dams may be more than 500 feet high. Some have a thickness less than one-fifth of their height.

GRAVITY DAMS. These structures, which are triangular in cross-section, rely on sheer weight for stability, so they require a large quantity of concrete. They can be used to span canyons that would be too wide for an arch dam (above). Although most gravity dams are straight, some are curved for added strength.

Parts of a Dam

Illustrated at right is a fictitious dam intended to show the functions of the most important parts. Seldom would a given dam have all of these features. Each of these features may be constructed in different ways, all serving the same general purpose.

Note: the sluiceway and penstock are built into the dam, and would not ordinarily be visible. They have been accentuated here to show how they work.

GATES AND VALVES. Many different styles of gates and valves are used to control the flow of water over or through a dam. These tainter gates (shown in red) control the flow of water over the spillway. Vertical lift gates (shown in blue) regulate the flow through the sluiceway and penstock.

SPILLWAY. A concrete structure that allows for passage of water over the dam. A spillway may or may not have gates to control water flow.

SCOUR PROTECTOR. A device, such as this "ski-jump" apron, for dissipating energy from the cascading water. Sometimes concrete baffles are installed in the tailwaters to serve as scour protectors. A deep *stilling pool* at the foot of the dam further slows the current.

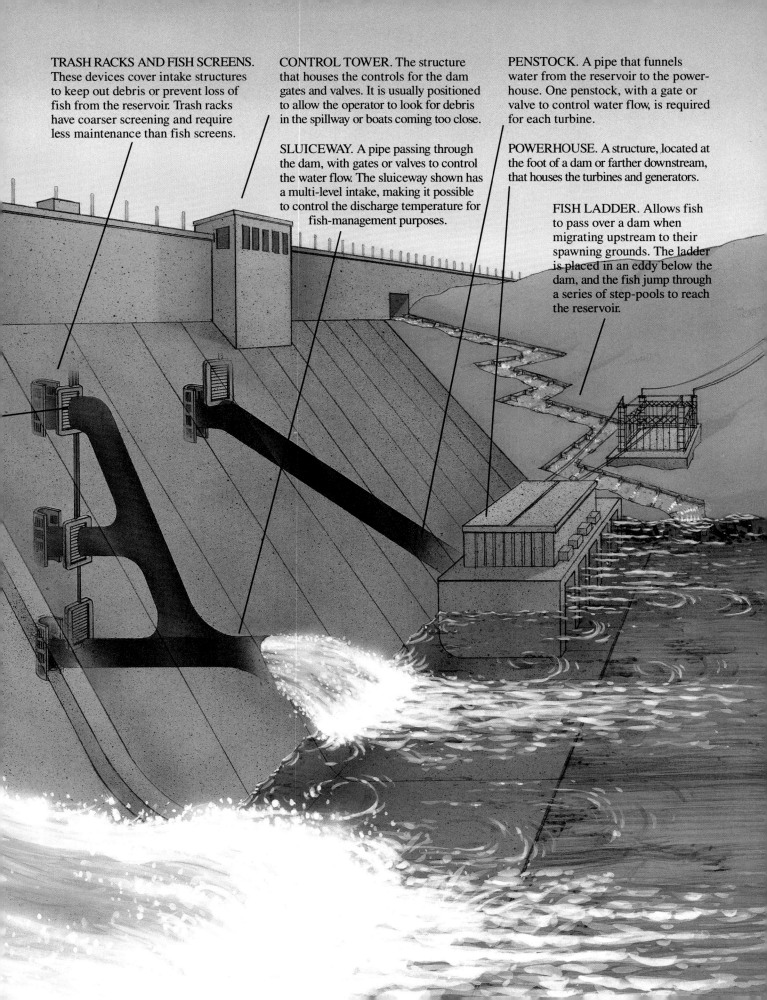

TRASH RACKS AND FISH SCREENS. These devices cover intake structures to keep out debris or prevent loss of fish from the reservoir. Trash racks have coarser screening and require less maintenance than fish screens.

CONTROL TOWER. The structure that houses the controls for the dam gates and valves. It is usually positioned to allow the operator to look for debris in the spillway or boats coming too close.

SLUICEWAY. A pipe passing through the dam, with gates or valves to control the water flow. The sluiceway shown has a multi-level intake, making it possible to control the discharge temperature for fish-management purposes.

PENSTOCK. A pipe that funnels water from the reservoir to the power-house. One penstock, with a gate or valve to control water flow, is required for each turbine.

POWERHOUSE. A structure, located at the foot of a dam or farther downstream, that houses the turbines and generators.

FISH LADDER. Allows fish to pass over a dam when migrating upstream to their spawning grounds. The ladder is placed in an eddy below the dam, and the fish jump through a series of step-pools to reach the reservoir.

Restored gravel pits are ideal for largemouth bass

Ponds & Pits

A staggering number of these small man-made lakes are found throughout the United States and Canada. Although precise numbers are not available, the combined surface area has been estimated at 20 million acres.

Ponds differ from pits in that they're constructed to hold water, mainly for agricultural or recreational purposes.

Pits, on the other hand, are simply depressions that fill with water after mining operations or other types of excavating activities have been completed.

As a rule, newer mine pits usually hold more fish than old ones. Federal legislation passed in 1977 requires that mine pits abandoned after that time be filled in and restored to their original state, unless they will be managed for fish and wildlife. As a result, many newer pits have irregular, gently sloping shorelines, riprapped banks to prevent erosion, islands or flats for structure or various types of fish shelters for extra cover.

The most common reasons for constructing ponds and pits include:

Ponds used for watering cattle may double as fishing waters

AGRICULTURAL USES. Farm ponds, sometimes called "stock tanks" in the western states, are the most numerous type of small man-made lake. Although most of these waters are built for the main purpose of watering livestock, many serve other purposes, including irrigation, erosion control and sport fishing. Thousands of ponds have been constructed solely for sport fishing, including many fee-fishing trout or catfish ponds.

Farm ponds are created by bulldozing or blasting a depression or, most commonly, by building an earthen dam across a small stream. These ponds measure from ¼ to several acres in size. As a rule, a good fishing pond should cover at least one acre. In the North, at least one-fourth of the pond must exceed 12 feet in depth to prevent frequent winterkills.

Aeration systems are sometimes installed in shallow ponds that will be stocked with fish. The aerators circulate the water in winter, preventing oxygen levels from dropping too low.

Most farm ponds are stocked with a combination of largemouth bass and bluegills. In theory, the bass prey on the young bluegills to keep their numbers in check. But if there are too few bass, the bluegill population explodes, resulting in a food shortage. The bluegills become stunted, and prey heavily on bass eggs and fry, further reducing bass numbers.

More than 2½ million farm ponds have been constructed through a U.S. Department of Agriculture cost-sharing program. The total number of farm ponds in the country is estimated to be 3 million.

GRAVEL OR ROCK PRODUCTION. Gravel pits and rock quarries usually fill with groundwater once they're abandoned. Their basins consist of porous materials, so their water level rises and falls with the water table.

Borrow pits are much like gravel pits or quarries, but tend to be a little shallower. Many borrow pits are located alongside highways, so they have straight shorelines and are often rectangular in shape. Fill used for highway construction is excavated, or "borrowed," from these pits and hauled to the construction site. To minimize transportation costs, the pits are usually located at regular intervals along the highway right-of-way.

Fill removed from borrow pits is used for building highways

21

Most coal-mining pits are long and narrow, with steep banks

Because the basins of these pits tend to be infertile, with no inflowing streams to furnish nutrients, they usually have clear water that lacks the fertility to produce large fish crops. The water stays clear despite heavy rains that murk up nearby lakes and streams.

The steep banks have little or no vegetation and, with the exception of rocks, there is no other natural cover for fish. Brush piles and old Christmas trees are sometimes sunk to provide additional cover.

Gravel pits and quarries are usually protected from the wind, so they stratify into distinct temperature layers in summer. Some of these waters have enough cold, oxygenated water in the depths to support trout. But in most pits and quarries, the depths lack oxygen; these waters are usually stocked with large-mouth bass and sunfish, and possibly catfish.

COAL MINING. When coal is strip-mined, the operation leaves narrow pits that can be more than 50 feet deep and a mile long. Strip pits are most common in western Kentucky, southern Indiana and

southern Illinois, but are found in many eastern and midwestern states.

When abandoned, these pits fill with water. Some are stocked with largemouth bass and bluegills, and a few with trout or catfish, soon after filling.

In pits that have not been restored (p. 20), acidic soil, steep sides and lack of cover may result in habitat that cannot support fish. But as the pit ages, the acidity decreases, slopes collapse and trees fall into the water. Only then can the pit be stocked.

PHOSPHATE MINING. Found mainly in Florida, phosphate pits are mined to produce phosphoric acid, one of the main ingredients in farm fertilizers.

After these pits fill, they're often colonized by a wide variety of fish species that enter through a network of drainage ditches. In some cases, these waters are stocked by private parties.

Common fish species in phosphate pits include large-mouth bass, bluegills, redear sunfish and catfish.

Phosphate pits are known for trophy largemouths, but the best pits are privately owned, so landowner permission is required to fish them.

Most pits of this type measure from 50 to 150 acres, with a few exceeding 1000 acres. The high phosphate concentration in the water causes dense algal blooms, but also produces large crops of baitfish. Mining operations leave the shoreline and bottom irregular, generally with maximum depths of 30 to 50 feet, resulting in ideal fish habitat.

Shallow phosphate pits may not be able to support gamefish. The wind stirs up highly fertile bottom sediments, keeping nutrients in suspension and often causing oxygen shortages.

IRON-ORE MINING. Abandoned iron-ore pits dot the landscape in northern Minnesota's Iron Range. Once mining operations cease, the basins gradually fill with ground-water, forming lakes ranging from 5 to more than 250 acres in size.

Many iron-ore pits are owned by the mining companies or located on other private lands, so they're closed to public use. But a fair number have been developed into public fishing lakes.

Some of these pits are very deep – more than 500 feet – with steep shorelines and extremely cold, clear, well-oxygenated water. Deep pits are often stocked with rainbow and brown trout, which usually inhabit only the upper-50-foot layer. Shallow pits generally hold bass and panfish.

Recently, commercial fish farmers have discovered that the icy waters of deep pits are ideal for raising trout and salmon. The fish are reared in net pens and fed a pelletized diet. They're harvested after 2 to 3 years and distributed to restaurants and grocery stores. In the future, fish farming in ore pits could become a major industry.

Phosphate pits often have heavy growths of floating plants or algae

Iron-ore pits may be hundreds of feet deep

Aftermath of the Johnstown flood

Problems Relating to Man-made Lakes

Although man-made lakes have greatly benefited society, they also cause some serious problems. Following are some of the most common ones:

INUNDATION OF FISH HABITAT. When a river or stream is flooded, populations of fish species that depend on current for successful spawning are gradually reduced. The new lakelike habitat may be better suited for slow-water species, such as largemouth bass and sunfish.

Flooding also displaces land animals, and in some cases, there is no other suitable habitat for them, so their populations diminish.

BLOCKING OF FISH RUNS. Migratory fish often swim upstream for miles, and sometimes hundreds of miles, to reach their spawning grounds. If a dam is built across a stream that supports such a run, the

Step-pools enable fish to ascend a fish ladder

fish are forced to spawn below the dam, where the habitat may or may not be suitable.

Various types of "fish ladders" have been designed to allow fish to pass over dams. But most ladders will not allow passage of very large fish. In some instances, fish must be trapped below dams and transported to their spawning grounds by truck.

The young of anadromous fish such as salmon must migrate downstream after hatching, and dams, especially those with power turbines, may block their way. On many western rivers, this poses an even more serious threat than blockage of upstream migration. To solve the problem, the young are often carried downstream on trucks or barges, or a bypass system is constructed so the fish can pass through or around the dam.

NITROGEN SUPERSATURATION. When water plunges over a dam, air, which is 78 percent nitrogen, is driven into the water, causing nitrogen supersaturation. Fish in the tailwaters take the nitrogen in through their gills, causing an excess of the gas in their blood. In years past, *gas-bubble disease* killed millions of trout and salmon in western streams. The problem has been reduced by construction of concrete slabs to smooth the flow of water as it spills over the dams.

EARTHQUAKES. The sheer weight of the water that fills a reservoir sometimes reactivates existing faults and causes a dramatic increase in seismic activity. Before construction of the Hoover Dam in 1935, for instance, no earth tremors had been experienced in the area for 15 years. But as gigantic Lake Mead filled, tremors began. Seismic activity peaked four years later with thousands of tremors occurring when the lake reached a depth of 475 feet.

SEDIMENTATION. Because reservoirs are fed by rivers with large flows, sediment accumulates rapidly. Sediment deposits first develop at the upper end of a reservoir and, over time, the sediment expands farther downstream. Many reservoirs built in the 1950s have lost 30 to 50 percent of their capacity because of sediment buildup.

The sediment not only reduces a lake's depth and leads to warming of the water, it covers the rocky or gravelly bottoms needed for food production and gamefish spawning. And sediments often carry pollutants that wind up in the lake bottom and lead to contamination of the fish. Because there is no practical way to remove this material, all reservoirs will fill in completely over time.

BOOM-BUST FISH CYCLE. When a reservoir starts filling, rising water drowns vegetation in the new basin. As the vegetation rots, nutrients released into the water trigger an explosion of plant and animal life. Fish populations expand quickly because of the abundance of food and lack of larger predator fish. This boom results in spectacular fishing, but usually lasts for only 5 to 20 years.

Braggin' board from the boom years – Lake Cumberland, Kentucky

Production of fish food gradually decreases as the vegetation disappears and nutrient levels wane. And siltation may stifle production of bottom organisms. The growth rate of gamefish decreases from lack of food; their survival rate from lack of cover.

Good fishing may continue for many years after the boom subsides, although catch rates are considerably lower than in the early years. The length of this intermediate period varies greatly, but is usually in the range of 20 to 60 years.

As a reservoir continues to age, conditions become more favorable for roughfish. A thick layer of rotting organic material forms on the bottom, often leading to low oxygen levels in the depths. And silt covers the firm bottom that many gamefish require for spawning. Anglers still catch some gamefish, but harvest is only 30 to 50 percent of that in the boom years.

SEVERE DRAWDOWNS. In desert lakes or any reservoirs subject to extreme water-level fluctuation, severe drawdowns usually mean trouble for gamefish populations. Spawning habitat is left high and dry, and there is often a shortage of food and cover.

PROBLEMS FOR PEOPLE. When large reservoirs are constructed, residents upstream of the dam are forced to relocate. Funds are generally provided to compensate for loss of their property, but people who are displaced often experience serious emotional problems.

DAM FAILURE. Although dam failure is extremely rare, the consequences are grave. The worst failure in U.S. history occurred in Johnstown, Pennsylvania in 1889, when the South Fork Dam on the Little Conemaugh River washed out from heavy rains, killing more than 2,000 people (opposite page). When a dam ruptures, the enormous wall of water washes away buildings, automobiles and anything else in its path.

Fishing Man-made Lakes

Desert Reservoirs

Gamefish now abound where cactuses once grew

Found mainly in the southwestern United States, desert reservoirs provide a reliable supply of water to cities and agricultural areas. Huge irrigation systems have made it possible to grow crops on millions of acres of land that previously were too dry during the growing season.

Most of these reservoirs are at least 100 feet deep, so they can store large volumes of water. But during a long-term drought, much of the water may drain off or evaporate, leaving barely enough to support fish life. Gamefish populations suffer when shallow food-production areas go dry.

When the reservoir refills, however, there is a boom in fish production, similar to what happens when a new reservoir fills (p. 25). Brush that develops on exposed shorelines during drought periods is flooded

when the water level rises, resulting in an abundance of food and cover for gamefish. Flooded trees and brush are especially important in lakes of this type, because the fluctuating water level limits growth of most aquatic plants.

Desert soils are typically rich in nutrients, so these reservoirs are usually quite fertile and productive. Because of their large watershed, they receive a heavy inflow of nutrients from surrounding lands.

The majority of desert lakes hold only warmwater fish species, primarily largemouth bass. Secondary species include white bass, crappies, catfish, smallmouth bass and sometimes striped bass or walleyes.

Deep desert reservoirs may have enough cold, well-oxygenated water to support trout.

The next world-record largemouth could easily come from a desert lake stocked with a combination of Florida bass and trout. The bass grow rapidly on a trout diet, and several 20-plus-pounders have already been taken from desert lakes in southern California.

Because desert reservoirs are usually found in regions with few other lakes, fishing pressure and other forms of water-based recreational usage are very high. Consequently, the fish tend to be finicky and difficult to catch, especially in lakes that have extremely clear water.

UPPER LAKE. The upper basin is shallower and has much more timber and brush than the lower basin. The timber has a chance to replenish itself when the basin goes dry for extended periods.

Case Study:

Elephant Butte Lake, New Mexico

Imaginative folks say the butte jutting from the water near the dam resembles the profile of an elephant's head – thus the lake's unusual name.

Elephant Butte

Construction of the Elephant Butte Dam across the Rio Grande River was completed in 1916. The lake is part of the Rio Grande Project, a water-control system intended to provide a reliable supply of irrigation water to parts of New Mexico and Texas.

Mexico is also guaranteed a portion of the Rio Grande's flow.

A power plant at the foot of the dam was added in 1940. Although the generators operate intermittently, depending on the amount of water being discharged, they are capable of producing enough hydroelectric power to supply a city of about 80,000.

Located between Albuquerque, New Mexico and El Paso, Texas, the lake is surrounded by mountainous, *semidesert* terrain dotted with creosote bushes, mesquite and prickly pear cactus.

Elephant Butte Lake consists of two main basins separated by a 4-mile-long narrows. There is a considerable difference in the character of the basins, as the photos above show.

The reservoir receives most of its water from snowmelt in the mountains. And like most desert lakes, it undergoes extreme water-level fluctuations, sometimes as much as 80 feet over the course of the year.

Long-term fluctuations resulting from drought conditions can be much greater. In the period from 1942 to 1951, the water level dropped about 145 feet, leaving the entire basin, with the exception of the main-river channel, dry. A drop of 60 feet below full-pool level is enough to drain the upper lake.

Besides flooded brush and timber, the lake contains little aquatic vegetation for gamefish cover, with the exception of milfoil and scattered beds of pondweeds. Local anglers sink Christmas trees in some of the coves, and rock outcrops on points and humps also provide cover.

Rated among the top fishing lakes in the Southwest, Elephant Butte is also a mecca for boaters and swimmers.

LOWER LAKE. The lower basin is deeper, wider, clearer and less fertile than the upper basin, with more rocky points and humps. The lower lake comprises 60 percent of the total acreage at full pool.

And the clear waters of the lower lake attract scuba divers.

The lake is best known for its plentiful crop of largemouth bass, which were native to the Rio Grande. White bass, catfish and crappies also occur naturally, and the lake has been stocked with smallmouth bass, walleyes and stripers, with the latter growing to spectacular size. In fact, the lake produced a 54-pound, 8-ounce striper, the current New Mexico record, in 1992.

Gamefish grow rapidly in the lake because the growing season is fairly long and food is plentiful. The surface temperature generally reaches 70°F in early June, and stays above 70 until late October. Shad, both gizzard and threadfin, are the major forage species, but gamefish also feed on yellow perch, sunfish, bullheads and a wide variety of minnows.

The fishing season for all species is continuous on Elephant Butte, and the bag limits are quite liberal. As in other regions where year-round bass fishing is allowed, the practice is controversial. We encourage anglers to gently release any bass caught around their spawning beds. This way, they will usually return to their nests and protect their young.

Elephant Butte Lake Physical Data

Year completed	1916
Dam type	gravity
Draw type	multi-level
Acreage	36,600
Average depth:	
upper lake	20 ft
lower lake	85 ft
Maximum depth:	
upper lake	62 ft
lower lake	197 ft
Water-level fluctuation:	
annual	20 ft
long term	149 ft
Water clarity:	
upper lake	6 in
lower lake	25 ft
Limits of thermocline:	highly variable
Trophic state:	
upper lake	eutrophic
lower lake	meso. to oligo.

Elephant Butte Reservoir

Upper Basin

The Narrows

Lower Basin

Dam

Rio Grande River

0   5   10
Scale in Miles

Albuquerque

NEW MEXICO

ARIZONA

Rio Grande River

Elephant Butte Reservoir

Truth or Consequences

El Paso

MEXICO   TEX.

Information and Services

General visitor information
T or C/Sierra County Chamber of Commerce
Box 31 - Truth or Consequences, NM 87901

Accommodations
Marina Suites Motel
Box 225 - Country Club Rd.
Elephant Butte, NM 87935

Dam Site Recreation Area
Box 778 - Engle Star Route
Truth or Consequences, NM 87901

Biologist
New Mexico Game & Fish Department
Villagra Building - Santa Fe, NM 87503

Guides
Buddy's Guide Service (Buddy Humphrey)
Box 25 - Elephant Butte, NM 87935

Bobby Brewster
Mescal Road - Elephant Butte, NM 87935

Desert Bass Fishing Guide Service (Dale Wagy)
Box 799 - Elephant Butte, NM 87935

SECONDARY POINTS in the canyons are good spawning areas for smallmouths and hold largemouths in spring and fall.

BACK ENDS of canyons are spawning areas for largemouths, catfish and white bass. Largemouths move back to milfoil flats in canyons in fall.

THE DEEP POOL above the dam produces stripers in winter and early spring, and a few largemouths and smallmouths from summer through winter.

Main river channel

MOUTHS of canyons are prime white bass areas in summer and fall. The fish roam a large area around the mouths and are often suspended.

LOWER-LAKE POINTS with rocky or gravelly bottoms and brush hold all species of gamefish from late spring through winter.

THE NARROWS between the upper and lower lake is the major striper-fishing area in fall. Stripers are drawn by shad moving out of the upper lake.

BRUSHY FLATS in the upper lake, especially where there is a rise, depression or tree clump, hold largemouths and catfish in summer and fall.

ARROYOS (dotted line) are small creek beds that run through the canyons. Largemouth bass use arroyos in early spring and fall; white bass and catfish, most of the year.

UPPER-LAKE POINTS with trees and brush, a hard bottom and deep water nearby are ideal for largemouths and catfish in summer and fall.

Elephant Butte Lake:

Largemouth Bass

The drastic difference in habitat between the upper and lower basins of Elephant Butte Lake means you'll have to tailor your largemouth-fishing strategy accordingly.

In early spring, for instance, the shallow upper lake warms much sooner, triggering spawning activity. Bass in the upper lake start to bite in mid-March, when the water reaches about 50°F. Spawning generally peaks around the full moon in April. In the deeper lower lake, the water doesn't warm enough for good fishing until mid-April, and spawning activity is heaviest around the full moon in May.

A few weeks before spawning, bass feed heavily on points at the mouths of or just inside the canyons where they will eventually spawn. Some fish hold in the arroyos leading into the canyons. Using a surface-temperature gauge, search for the warmest water to locate the active bass.

In shallow, brushy cover, try flippin' a jig-and-pig (p. 37). Be sure to use one with a stout hook that won't bend when you horse the fish out of the cover. On cleaner, deeper structure, slow-hop a jig-and-pig, one with a thinner wire hook for better penetration. Slow-rolling (p. 57) a tandem-blade spinnerbait works well in either shallow or deep water.

For flippin' in heavy cover, use a 7½-foot, heavy-power, fast-action flippin' stick and a baitcasting reel spooled with 25-pound mono. A 6-foot, medium-heavy baitcasting outfit with 17-pound mono is adequate for spinnerbait fishing or working a jig-and-pig in deeper water.

Shallow, protected canyons warm earliest and draw the bulk of the spawners, although a few fish spawn on main-lake reefs and points.

The secret to catching spawning bass is to find their beds. Look for beds at the back ends of the canyons, usually near some type of cover, such as mesquite, rocks or stumps.

Move slowly with your trolling motor, wearing polarized sunglasses to help spot fish on the beds. When you see a fish, hold still and slowly back your boat

Important Types of Timber and Brush for Largemouths

SALT CEDAR. This is the most common type of flooded brush in Elephant Butte and the primary cover for largemouth bass. It holds fish throughout the year. The branches are much straighter than those of mesquite (right).

MESQUITE. These bushes, which have knobby branches with many sharp bends, are found on a gravel bottom, so they draw bass around spawning time. In late summer and early fall, bass hold in mesquite clumps among the salt cedar.

COTTONWOOD. These tall, thick-trunked trees are easy to identify because of their large size. Bass may build spawning beds on roots of trees in water less than 5 feet deep. In fall, bass may suspend in trees in deeper water.

LURES for largemouth bass include: (1) Poe's Super Cedar, series 400, a deep-diving crankbait; (2) Smithwick Devil's Horse, a propbait; (3) Bomber Popper, a chugger; (4) Hopkins Smoothie, a jigging spoon; (5) Bulldog Hawg Dog, a tandem-blade spinnerbait; (6) Ditto Baby Fat Grub, Texas-rigged with a size 1/0 offset hook and a split shot; (7) Stanley Jig with pork trailer; (8) Hale's Craw Worm, Texas-rigged; (9) Fatzee tube bait, Texas-rigged with hook point exposed.

away. Cast a "finesse bait" (p. 39), such as a weenie worm, so it settles into the nest and let it rest motionless for a minute or two. Twitch it occasionally until it pulls away from the nest, then reel in and cast again. Tempting the fish to bite may be difficult.

The difference in spawning times at opposite ends of the lake means you should never have to fish for post-spawn bass, those that are recuperating from the rigors of spawning and very difficult to catch. When bass at the upper end have finished spawning, those at the lower end are just starting. When those at the lower end have finished, those at the upper end have recuperated and started to feed.

Once the fish regain their strength and leave the spawning areas, they begin feeding heavily on shad, so angling success picks up. The shallow, brushy cover in the upper lake produces plenty of good-sized largemouths in summer. Flippin' is the best way to reach bass in the brushy tangle. You'll probably have better success using a jig with a soft-plastic lizard or crawworm, or a Texas-rigged plastic worm, than a jig-and-pig. Spinnerbaits also produce, but you should retrieve them faster than in spring.

The best summertime spots in the lower lake are rocky points and humps with brushy cover, but you can find fish on most any brushy structure from 5 to 15 feet deep. Bass in the lower lake don't run quite as large, and they tend to roam about more in search of shad. Your odds are best early (before 9) and late (after 7) in the day. Then, topwaters worked rapidly across the surface and crankbaits are good choices.

In midday, try jig fishing or split-shotting with a finesse bait. In cloudy or windy weather, the fish bite all day.

You can use the same baitcasting outfit for topwaters and crankbaits as you do for spinnerbaits, but some experts advocate a softer fiberglass rod. This way, you'll lose fewer fish because the rod will bend before the hooks tear out. To cast lightweight split-shot rigs with finesse baits, use a 6½-foot, medium-power spinning outfit with 8-pound mono.

By mid-August, cooling water draws largemouths onto milfoil flats at the back ends of lower-lake canyons. The action is usually fastest in midday.

Propbaits worked with a twitch-and-pause retrieve are excellent fall producers. Let the lure rest for up to 10 seconds when it reaches a stick-up or any object that could hold a bass. Another proven method is split-shotting with finesse baits along edges and openings in the milfoil beds.

Largemouths start moving deeper around mid-November as the water continues to cool. They're much less active, but still catchable. Look for them on any deep structure in the lower lake, usually at depths of 20 to 45 feet.

The best way to catch bass once they go deep is slow-dragging a finesse bait or a live crayfish or shad on a split-shot rig. Or try jigging vertically with a jigging spoon, using a stiff 5½-foot baitcasting outfit and 17-pound mono. This winter pattern holds until the water begins to warm in early March.

Flippin' into Heavy Cover

1. CAST your lure out about the same distance you will be flippin'. You must start with the lure well out in front of you to get the pendulum motion started.

2. PULL the lure out of the water and draw it back toward the boat by lifting your rod tip while pulling on the line with your other hand. Be sure the reel spool is engaged.

3. LOWER your rod tip as the lure begins to swing past you. Continue to hold the line with your other hand so the lure can reach the back of its arc without touching the water.

4. RAISE your rod tip and, at the same time, tug the line slightly with your other hand to propel the lure toward the target. Keep it just high enough so the lure clears the water.

5. BRING the hand holding the line back toward the rod, allowing the weight of the lure to pull the line through the guides. Stop feeding line when the lure reaches the precise target.

6. SET the lure into the water with minimal splash. Lower the rod as the lure sinks so it doesn't swing toward the boat.

Elephant Butte Lake:
Smallmouth Bass

With so much attention focused on largemouths, many anglers do not realize that Elephant Butte sports an excellent population of smallmouths, with plenty of fish in the 3- to 4½-pound class.

You'll find the majority of smallmouths in the lower 10 miles of the lake, where the water is clearest and coolest in summer. As a rule, they'll be near some type of rocky structure.

When the water temperature approaches 60°F, which is usually in mid- to late April, smallmouths move into their spawning areas. Rocky shorelines in the canyons warm first and draw early spawners, but many fish spawn later on rocky shores of the main lake. The best spawning areas are no more than 6 feet deep, with scattered boulders to protect the nests from wind and predators.

Smallmouths spawn at water temperatures in the mid 60s. Total time between the first spawning activity in the creek arms and the last activity in the main lake ranges from 3 to 5 weeks.

When smallmouths concentrate around their spawning areas, you can easily catch them by fan-casting small topwaters and retrieving with a twitch-and-pause motion. Or use a finesse bait (opposite page) on a split-shot rig and work it with a very slow lift-and-drop retrieve over visible beds or through the areas around them. Some anglers let the lure rest right on a bed for several minutes, giving it only an occasional wiggle. When fishing topwaters or finesse baits, use the same outfits as you would when fishing largemouths with these lures (p. 36).

Springtime fishing is best when the water is warming. The action is fastest early and late in the day, especially when using topwaters.

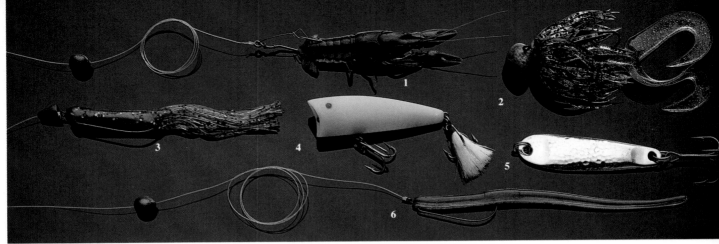

LURES AND BAITS for smallmouths include: (1) crayfish on split-shot rig with weedless hook; (2) Yamamoto Spider Jig; (3) Fatzee tube bait on offset hook with exposed point and bullet sinker; (4) Rebel Pop-R, a chugger; (5) Hopkins Spoon, a jigging spoon; (6) Roboworm, a weenie worm, Texas-rigged on offset hook with split shot.

Finesse Baits and How to Fish Them

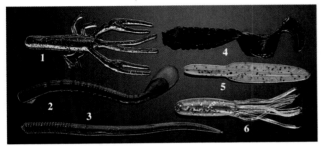

POPULAR FINESSE BAITS include: (1) small crawworm, (2) paddletail worm, (3) weenie worm, (4) curly-tail grub, (5) eel-tail grub, (6) small tube bait.

INCH the lure along slowly with a twitch-and-pause retrieve. On the twitch, the lure rises; on the pause, it sinks slowly since there is no weight on the lure itself.

Once spawning has been completed, you can easily catch nest-guarding males, which are very aggressive. Catching females, however, is next to impossible for a week or two after they spawn. But since they don't all spawn at once, you should be able to find some catchable females through the entire spawning period.

After smallmouths leave their spawning areas, they move to rocky points and isolated rocky humps that top out at about 5 feet and have scattered bushes. In low-light periods, especially in early morning, the fish often feed right on top of the structure. Under bright conditions, they retreat to depths of 10 to 15 feet and do less feeding. Split-shotting with finesse baits is the most productive summertime technique.

As the water cools in fall, the fish spend less and less time in the shallows. By early October, a few smallmouths remain on tops of the points and humps where they were in summer, but most of them have moved to depths of 15 to 25 feet. By mid-November, however, smallmouths spend practically all their time in deeper water. Finesse baits work equally well in fall.

Fall smallmouth fishing is best during periods of stable weather. You can catch fish any time of day, but cloudy weather or a slight chop seems to improve the action.

The water temperature normally drops below 50°F by the middle of January, slowing smallmouth activity to the lowest level of the year. Most of the fish hold at depths of 20 to 30 feet on rocky points and humps that break very sharply into deep water. Often smallmouths suspend just off the structure, where they're difficult to find and catch.

Although fishing is usually tough during the winter, slow-dragging finesse baits or vertically jigging with spoons may take a few smallmouths. Use the same outfit for vertically jigging as you would for largemouths (p. 36).

But if spoons or finesse baits don't produce, try a split-shot rig with a live shad or crayfish. Hook a 2- to 3-inch crayfish through the tail with a size 1/0 weedless hook and retrieve it very slowly. Shad from 3 to 5 inches long are about right for smallmouths; fish them as you would for stripers (p. 43). For live-bait fishing, use a 6-foot, medium-power spinning outfit with 8- to 12-pound mono. These live-bait techniques will take either smallmouths or largemouths year-round.

Elephant Butte Lake:

Striped Bass

The huge stripers in Elephant Butte draw fishermen from all over the Southwest. Each year, anglers do battle with dozens of fish in the 35- to 50-pound class. In 1992, the lake yielded the state-record striper, weighing 54 pounds, 8 ounces.

Although the striper population is not large, you have a reasonable chance of connecting if you fish in known concentration areas at the right time of year.

You can catch a few stripers through the coldest part of the winter, but the action really picks up in mid-March, when the fish begin to congregate above the dam to spawn. Small groups consisting of a female and one or two males cruise the shorelines or roam expanses of open water at depths of 20 to 25 feet.

When the water temperature reaches 55°F, usually in late March, stripers begin to spawn along rocky

LURES for striped bass include: (1) Cordell Pencil Popper, a chugger; (2) Cordell Redfin, a floating minnow plug; (3) horsehead jig tipped with a soft-plastic curlytail; (4) live shad, rigged on a size 2/0 hook.

THREADFIN VS. GIZZARD SHAD. Threadfin shad (top) do not work as well for bait as gizzard shad (bottom). Gizzard shad are hardier, and grow to a larger size. You can distinguish between the two by differences in coloration. The gizzard shad has a blackish margin on the tail; the threadfin, yellowish.

shorelines in the vicinity of the dam. Spawning activity continues into early May. But striper eggs require moving water to hatch, so no young are produced in the lake environment. Consequently, the fishery depends entirely on stocking.

Once stripers leave their spawning areas, they begin to appear on large lower-lake flats that top out at 40 to 60 feet adjacent to water at least 80 feet deep. These areas hold fish from the middle of May through early September.

By far the most effective striper technique – one that works any time of year – is slow-trolling, either with live shad or horsehead jigs with 4- to 5-inch curlytails. Most anglers opt for the latter because live shad are not available at bait shops; you have to net your own. But shad are tough to match as bait. In winter and spring, use shad from 4 to 6 inches long; in summer and fall, 7 to 11 inches.

In spring and fall, when stripers are found from the surface to a depth of 25 feet, you can rig the shad on balloon lines, down lines, or unweighted "flat lines" (opposite page). In summer, stripers hold just beneath the thermocline, usually at depths of 40 to 60 feet, so you'll have to rely mainly on down lines. Fishing can be tough in winter, but you may be able to catch a few fish near the bottom on balloon lines and down lines at depths of 25 to 40 feet.

Another good summertime technique, especially in early morning and in cloudy weather, is surface fishing with big minnow plugs and pencil poppers on main-lake points and shallow humps adjacent to deep water. Fish a minnow plug with a slow, steady retrieve so it creates a prominent wake; a pencil popper, with continuous twitches.

Fishing peaks in late November, when stripers are drawn to the narrows by schools of shad forced out of the upper lake by the cooling water. Look for shad schools with a graph; the stripers won't be far away.

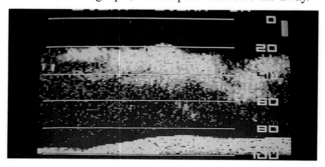

Huge shad schools appear as dense clouds on a graph

The most popular way to fish the narrows is casting or slow-trolling with horsehead jigs. When casting, count the jig down to the depth of the fish before beginning your retrieve. Live shad and surface lures also work well in fall. When the water temperature in the narrows drops below 50°F, usually in mid-January, the shad move into the main lake and the stripers follow.

A 7-foot, heavy-power, fiberglass baitcasting outfit works well for all types of striper fishing mentioned. A fiberglass rod will take more punishment than a graphite, and sensitivity is not important in these fishing methods. Spool your reel with 14- to 30-pound mono, depending on the thickness of the cover.

As a rule, stripers bite best early and late in the day. In fall, however, they feed all day long, and in winter, they sometimes bite at night. Stable weather with a light breeze is generally better than stormy or calm conditions.

Multi-line Trolling for Stripers

This technique enables you to cover a range of depths while keeping some of your lines far enough behind the boat that you won't spook the stripers.

If desired, you can attach side planers (p. 91) to some of your lines so they run as much as 50 feet to the side of the boat, further reducing spooking.

PUSH the hook through a shad's nostrils. Use a 1/0 or 2/0 hook for 4- to 6-inchers; a 3/0 or 4/0 for 7- to 11-inchers. This hooking method keeps the shad lively.

PEG a 2- to 3-ounce egg sinker onto each down line, about 4 feet above the hook. Pegging the sinker, rather than tying in a swivel, eliminates knots and reduces line breakage.

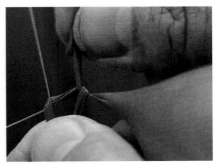

RIG balloon lines using an overhand knot to tie the balloon at the proper depth. Add a large split shot 4 feet above the hook. To change depth, slide the balloon up or down the line.

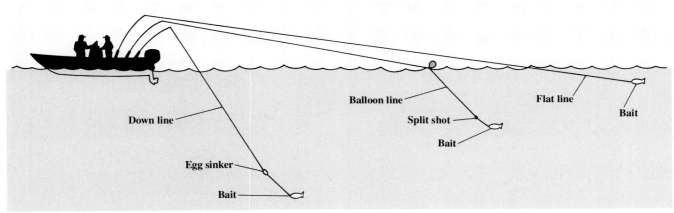

COVER a wide depth range and reduce spooking by using a combination of down lines, balloon lines and flat lines. Down lines run deepest; flat lines, which are not weighted, run shallowest. Down lines trail just behind the boat; balloon lines, about 50 feet back; and flat lines, at least 75 feet back. Stagger the distances to avoid tangling.

Tips for Multi-line Trolling

USE a bow-mounted electric motor so you can troll quietly and avoid spooking the fish. Trolling in an S-pattern also helps; this way, the trailing lines do not follow directly in the boat's wake.

CAST a large floating minnow plug or horsehead jig toward shore as you troll. Angle your casts ahead of the boat and retrieve the plug so it makes a noticeable wake. This technique increases your zone of coverage even more.

Elephant Butte Lake:

Catfish

Cats abound in Elephant Butte; when conditions are right, it's not unusual to land a hundred a day. Channel catfish are most numerous, but the lake also holds plenty of flatheads and blues. Flatheads grow larger than the others; the lake record is 79 pounds.

Channels from 1 to 3 pounds are the main target of anglers. Most of the flatheads and blues are taken on trotlines, although anglers also catch a few blues. Only angling techniques are covered here.

Catfish are found throughout the lake, but the upper basin offers the most consistent fishing. Cats in the lower lake use deeper water, so they're somewhat harder to find.

In late April, catfish begin gathering near their spawning areas in the shallow back ends of canyons. Spawning takes place at water temperatures from 70 to 75°F, usually sometime in June. They build their nests on wooded, brushy knolls, generally in 2 to 6 feet of water.

Arroyos in the back ends of canyons often load up with cats at spawning time; the fish use these deeper channels as migration routes.

After spawning has been completed, you can find cats in the upper lake at depths of 18 to 25 feet and occasionally as deep as 35. Look for them in that depth range in arroyos, on wooded flats and on points, especially those at the mouths of spawning canyons. The prime spots generally have plenty of woody cover.

Cats bite well through the summer and fall, with the peak time from early September to early December. The fish stay in the same general areas through the winter, often moving a bit deeper. But they're much less active than in summer and fall.

Chumming for Catfish

Chumming (below) is the key to catching catfish at any time of year. Mix the chum several days in advance to give the grain enough time to ferment.

In spring, spread the chum over an area about 50 feet in diameter, and anchor your boat alongside it. Then, cast the bait into the chum zone and fish it right on the bottom. In summer and fall, when the fish are deeper, chum a much smaller area and tie up to a tree right over it. Lower the bait straight down to the bottom, then reel it up a little.

Weather and time of day have little to do with catfishing success, particularly when you're chumming. The chum seems to activate fish that previously weren't feeding.

Chum Recipe:

1   50-pound bag of wheat, mylo or cracked corn

3   cups sugar

Water

Fill three five-gallon buckets two-thirds full of wheat, mylo or cracked corn. Add one cup of sugar to each bucket. Add water until the level is a few inches above the grain. Cover the buckets and allow two days for the grain to absorb the water. Then, refill the buckets so the water level is again a few inches above the grain; reseal. Allow the grain to ferment five days at a temperature of 75°F; three days at 90.

How to Chum Catfish

CHUM in early morning, using about a gallon of the mixture in each spot you intend to fish during the day. Give the chum an hour or so to work before you start fishing.

TIE OFF to a tree in or alongside the area that was chummed. Look for a distinctive tie-off tree before you start chumming. Then, you can easily find the same tree when you return.

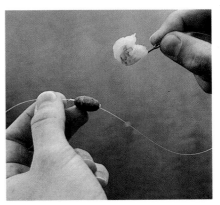

BAIT UP with a piece of shrimp, cut shad or hot dog. Bury a heavy size 1/0 hook inside the bait so the point is not exposed. Otherwise, the fish might spit the bait.

PLACE your rods in rod holders. This enables you to fish with two lines at the same time, and makes it easier to see bites, which can be surprisingly subtle.

HORSE the fish out of the cover using a 6- to 7-foot, medium-heavy baitcasting outfit and 20-pound mono. If you let the fish run, it may swim around a branch.

45

Elephant Butte Lake:
White Bass

As in most other man-made lakes with a healthy shad crop, a flock of diving gulls probably means there's a school of rampaging white bass just below. It pays to be on the lookout for gull activity, which can happen anytime from summer through fall.

The whites in Elephant Butte run good size – from 1 to 2 pounds, with an occasional 3. When they're schooled up, you can easily catch a limit of 40 in an hour or two.

Beginning in mid-March, whites move into the back ends of canyons where they'll spawn when the water temperature reaches the upper 50s. Just before spawning time, you'll find them at depths of 15 feet or less; at spawning time, 8 or less. They often concentrate near clumps of flooded brush, where you can catch them on jigs, vibrating plugs and crankbaits. You can also twitch a minnow plug along the surface or fish near bottom with a live shad on a split-shot rig.

The fish stay in the canyons until the water temperature reaches the upper 60s, which is normally in late May. Then they begin moving into the outer fringes of the canyons or just into the main lake, where they will stay the rest of the year. They seldom roam far from their spawning canyons.

Look for white bass on points at the mouths of canyons or in the arroyos leading out of the canyons. Early and late in the day, you'll find them at depths of 8 to 10 feet; in midday, 30 to 40 feet. This pattern persists until mid-November.

When the fish are in the shallows, try casting to them with a vibrating plug. You can make long casts and cover a lot of water quickly. Vibrating plugs also work well for fishing the "jumps" (p. 90), as do chuggers, jigs and tailspins. When the fish go deep in midday, hover over them and vertically jig with a jigging spoon.

Another productive technique is night fishing with live shad or small minnows, particularly from late April to early September. A graph comes in handy for this type of fishing; simply lower your bait to the depth where you see the bass. Lights attract shad at night, so anglers looking for white bass often fish around lighted marinas (right) or set out floating crappie lights. Live shad also work well during the day.

For live-bait, jig or minnow-plug fishing, select a 6- to 7-foot, medium-power spinning outfit with 6- to 10-pound mono. For jigging spoons, crankbaits, vibrating plugs or popping plugs, use a 5½- to 6-foot, medium-power baitcasting rig with 8- to 12-pound mono.

As the water cools in late fall, white bass start to move deeper and anglers have a tough time finding them. Very few are caught from early December through mid-February.

Whites bite best during periods of stable weather, preferably with a light chop on the water. Rising water temperatures seem to turn them on in spring.

LURES include: (1) Heddon Tiny Chugger; (2) Bomber Long A, a floating minnow plug; (3) Bagley Small Fry Shad, a medium-running crankbait; (4) Hopkins Spoon, a jigging spoon; (5) Bill Lewis Mini-Trap, a vibrating plug; (6) live shad on split-shot rig with size 1 hook; (7) Mann's Little George, a tailspin; (8) Mister Twister Meeny jig.

Tips for Catching White Bass

LOOK for gulls diving into the water to feed on shad injured by white bass. Keep your distance from the school and cast to them with a jig, tailspin, chugger or vibrating plug.

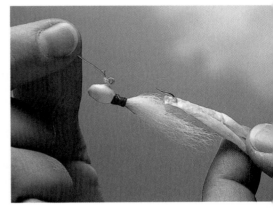

TIP your jig with a belly strip from a white bass when the action slows down. The strips, which are about ¼ inch wide and 1 to 1½ inches long, attract the less aggressive fish.

MARINA LIGHTS draw white bass at night. The lights attract small insects and plankton, which bring in shad and, before long, the whites follow. Simply lower a shad or live minnow, either on a ⅛-ounce jig or a split-shot rig, over the side and work it right below the boat. Try different depths until you find the fish; normally, they'll be at 15 to 20 feet.

Flatland Reservoirs

These shallow, fertile reservoirs rank among the country's top trophy bass waters

The flat to gently rolling terrain around these lakes means the water is relatively shallow, the main basin wide and the creek arms short.

Some flatland reservoirs are more than 100 feet deep near the dam, but the major part of their basins have depths of only 30 to 60 feet. As a result, they're best suited to warmwater fish species, mainly largemouth bass, crappies, sunfish, catfish and white bass. Many deeper lakes of this type have been stocked with striped bass or hybrids.

Because the surrounding land is mainly agricultural, these lakes receive large quantities of nutrients, meaning abundant crops of baitfish (primarily shad) and fast-growing gamefish. But the high fertility also means a lack of coldwater fish, because oxygen levels in the depths fall too low in summer.

Plankton blooms resulting from the fertile water, combined with silt kept in suspension by the mixing effect of the wind, usually keep the water murky.

Timber and brush provide the main cover for fish, especially in the early stages of the reservoir's life. The shallow creek arms are often heavily timbered, as are shoreline points and flats, unless the basin has been clear-cut. But as these lakes age and the woody cover disappears, weeds become more important as cover.

Flatland reservoirs generally undergo less severe water-level fluctuations than most other types of reservoirs. Consequently, aquatic plants become established more easily than in lakes that undergo greater fluctuations.

Case Study:

Richland-Chambers Reservoir, Texas

Impounded by a 6-mile earthen dam in 1987, Richland-Chambers is one of the country's youngest man-made lakes. And, as happens in most youthful reservoirs, the fish population is booming – a phenomenon that will probably continue for at least a decade.

Although the lake was created primarily to supply water to the Fort Worth area, it also reduces flooding of downstream areas. In addition, planners took fishing into consideration during the design phases, leaving a great deal of timber and brush in the shallows to provide spawning cover for adult fish and hiding cover for juveniles. There is also a large expanse of open water that is ideal for sailing and waterskiing.

A typical "flatland" reservoir, Richland-Chambers is surrounded by fertile farm fields and pastureland. The water is shallow and high in nutrients, meaning rapid fish growth. But the high fertility also means low oxygen levels in the depths. In midsummer, the oxygen level in the upper lake is too low to support fish life below 20 feet; in the lower lake, below 40 feet.

Because the surrounding land is so flat, the lake frequently gets buffeted by high winds, stirring up silt and keeping the water clarity low.

The lake produced a surprising number of large fish immediately after impoundment. Richland and

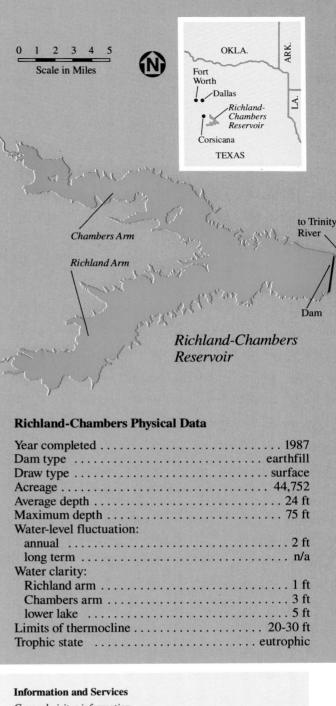

OKLA.

Fort
Worth
Dallas
*Richland-Chambers
Reservoir*
Corsicana

TEXAS

ARK.

LA.

to Trinity
River

Chambers Arm

Richland Arm

Dam

Richland-Chambers Reservoir

Richland-Chambers Physical Data

Year completed	1987
Dam type	earthfill
Draw type	surface
Acreage	44,752
Average depth	24 ft
Maximum depth	75 ft
Water-level fluctuation:	
annual	2 ft
long term	n/a
Water clarity:	
Richland arm	1 ft
Chambers arm	3 ft
lower lake	5 ft
Limits of thermocline	20-30 ft
Trophic state	eutrophic

Chambers creeks had significant populations of cat-fish and white bass before the lake filled, good-sized bass came from the many farm ponds that were flooded, and crappies migrated downstream from other impoundments.

Besides the native fish, the lake has been stocked with Florida bass and additional channel and blue catfish. Florida or "coppernose" bluegills (named for the copper-colored patch on the forehead) have also been stocked, but few are caught by anglers, probably because they're heavily preyed upon by cat-fish and largemouths. The primary forage fish are threadfin and gizzard shad.

Largemouths are the target of most Richland-Chambers fishermen, with crappies running a close second. Catfish are caught primarily on multiple-hook trot-lines, although there is some angling.

At present, there are more than a dozen boat land-ings on the lake, but no resort facilities. A large marina complex is being planned, however.

Information and Services

General visitor information
Corsicana Chamber of Commerce
120 N. 12th St. - Corsicana, TX 75110

Biologist
Texas Parks & Wildlife Department
Rt. 10 Box 1043 - Tyler, TX 75707

Guides
Don Combs
Rt. 6 Box 224C - Corsicana, TX 75110

Allen's Guide Service
Rt. 6 Box 175 AB - Corsicana, TX 75110

Bill Law
Rt. 1 Box 1694 - Streetman, TX 75859

Accommodations
Oak Cove Inn
Box 111 - Corsicana, TX 75110

Main river channel

BRUSHY CREEK ARMS with flowing water are the major spawning areas for crappies and white bass. They also hold bass in spring and fall.

ROADBEDS offer a hard bottom and deep water in the adjacent ditches. They attract largemouths, and sometimes white bass and crappies, in summer.

WOODED COVES are the main spawning areas for largemouth bass and catfish. They also draw some crappies in spring. Bass return to these areas in fall.

WOODED POINTS make prime cover for largemouths, crappies, white bass and catfish. They hold some fish most of the year.

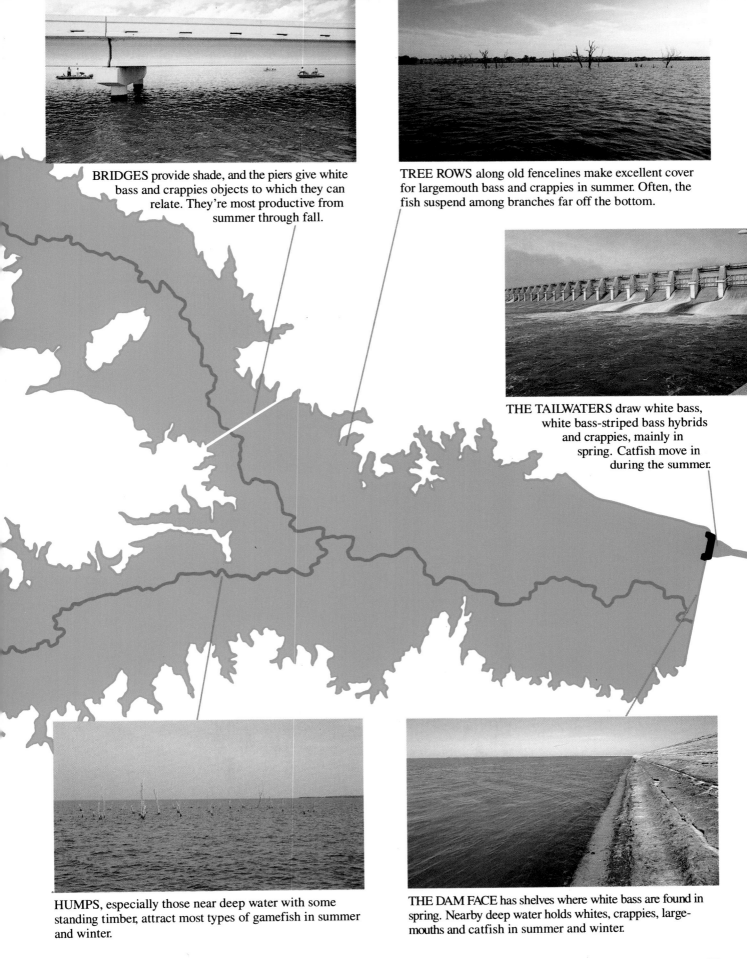

BRIDGES provide shade, and the piers give white bass and crappies objects to which they can relate. They're most productive from summer through fall.

TREE ROWS along old fencelines make excellent cover for largemouth bass and crappies in summer. Often, the fish suspend among branches far off the bottom.

THE TAILWATERS draw white bass, white bass-striped bass hybrids and crappies, mainly in spring. Catfish move in during the summer.

HUMPS, especially those near deep water with some standing timber, attract most types of gamefish in summer and winter.

THE DAM FACE has shelves where white bass are found in spring. Nearby deep water holds whites, crappies, largemouths and catfish in summer and winter.

Richland-Chambers Reservoir:

Largemouth Bass

Trophy largemouth are becoming routine on Richland-Chambers. And they'll surely be even more common in years to come. With the lake still in its "boom" cycle and well stocked with Florida bass, it's only a matter of time before anglers begin weighing in "teen" fish.

In late February, bass begin moving into creek arms off the upper ends of the main creek channels. A few warm days raise the water temperature into the mid-50s and draw the fish onto 5- to 10-foot timbered flats. The lower end of the lake warms more slowly, so bass move into those creek arms 2 to 3 weeks later.

Spawning begins when the water temperature reaches the low 60s. Look for spawners in 1 to 5 feet of water on a firm, sandy bottom with brushy cover. By late April, all bass throughout the lake have spawned.

During the pre-spawn and spawning period, cast spinnerbaits into the shallows and use a slow-roll retrieve (p. 57), pausing to let them helicopter alongside brush piles and logs. Another good technique is twitching a floating minnow plug through the heavy cover.

Bass stay in the creek arms for 10 days to 2 weeks after spawning, but the females are tough to catch.

You can take a few fish by casting a crankbait, vibrating plug or Texas-rigged worm, lizard or crawworm onto timbered flats from 5 to 15 feet deep.

By early June, most of the bass have moved back to the main lake. You'll find them at depths of 12 to 20 feet on timbered flats and humps along the main creek channels, along fencerows and submerged road ditches and around points. They also move into the many flooded stock tanks (man-made ponds for watering cattle, p. 56). The fish are never far from timber or brush.

The surface temperature reaches the 80s by mid-July, forcing bass to retreat to depths of 15 to 25 feet. But they won't be far from their early summer locations. They stay in these spots until early October.

Texas-rigged worms, lizards and crawworms continue to produce through the summer and into fall. If the bottom is clean enough, try a Carolina rig instead. The lure will drop more slowly, often triggering inactive fish. Another good summertime technique is fishing the brushy cover on deep stock tanks by vertically jigging with a spoon or tailspin, or casting with a jig-and-pig or Texas-rigged worm (p. 56).

By mid-October, most bass have moved into secondary creek arms. You'll catch them at depths of 15 feet or less using crankbaits, spinnerbaits and topwaters such as propbaits, buzzbaits and chuggers. By early November, fish begin moving into the main creek arms. They often suspend 15 to 20 feet down on heavily timbered flats adjacent to the main creek

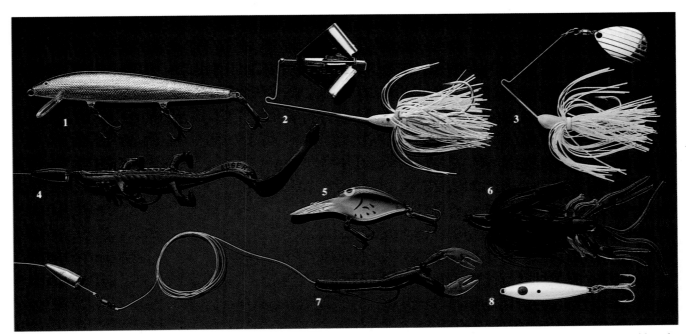

LURES for largemouths include: (1) A. C. Shiner, a floating minnow plug; (2) Bulldog Buzzbait; (3) Stanley Thumper, a single-spin spinnerbait; (4) 6-inch Mann's Auger Lizard, rigged Texas-style; (5) Storm Rattlin' Flat Wart, a deep-diving crankbait; (6) Penetrator Jig, a rubber-legged brush-guard jig, with Guido Bug trailer; (7) Stanley Hale's Craw Worm, rigged Carolina-style; (8) Mann's Mann-O-Lure, a jigging spoon.

channels, but you can draw them up with the top-waters just mentioned, or go down to them with jigs, crankbaits or spinnerbaits retrieved slowly.

When the water temperature drops to the low 50s, usually in late December, bass descend into depths of 25 to 40 feet in the main creek channels. Fishing is slow in winter, but you can catch a few fish by vertically jigging a spoon or tailspin to catch bass suspended 10 to 20 feet deep around flooded trees along the channel edges.

A 6- to 7-foot, medium to medium-heavy baitcasting outfit works well for all the techniques mentioned above. Because of the heavy timber and brush, most anglers use 17- to 20-pound (or heavier) line. Use lighter line, about 14-pound test, only when casting crankbaits and minnow plugs in lighter cover.

Shallow-water bass tend to bite best on overcast days with a light breeze. In this kind of weather, fishing is usually good all day long. On calm, sunny days, you'll catch more fish early and late in the day.

Deep-water bass are most active on sunny, breezy days, except in summer, when cloudy weather is best. You'll normally catch more fish in the afternoon than in the morning.

How to Find and Fish Stock Tanks

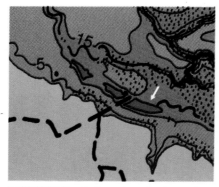  

LOCATE flooded stock tanks (arrow) on a detailed reservoir map. Richland-Chambers has hundreds of these tanks.

STOCK TANKS are often surrounded by trees (left) because of the availability of water. After the reservoir fills, the row of trees outlining a stock tank (right) can help you find it in a hurry.

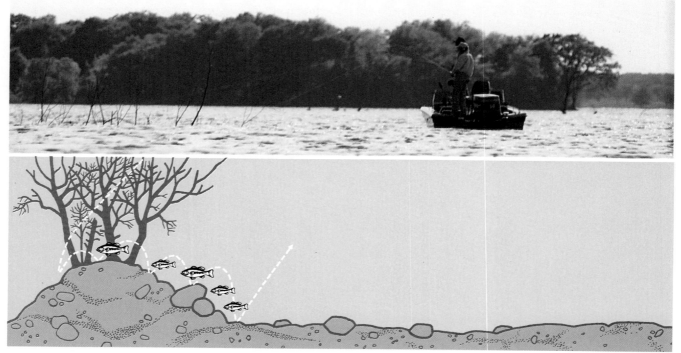

POSITION your boat outside the dam to fish shallow stock tanks. Cast over the dam and work your lure across the top and down the outside edge, the places where bass normally lie. On deeper tanks, vertically jig over heavy timber.

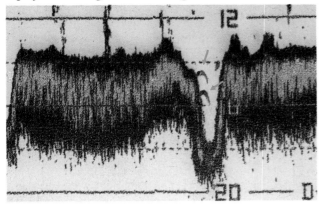

LOOK for ditches alongside submerged roadbeds. Bass (arrows) usually lie along the slopes of the ditches, as shown on this graph tape, but they may feed right on the roadbed early and late in the day or in cloudy weather.

BUCKBRUSH provides excellent pre- and post-spawn bass cover. It grows in shallow creek arms with firm bottoms, near the places where bass spawn. Bass usually hold in the thickest part of the clump.

CEDAR TREES have dense branches that offer perfect cover for bass, especially in spring and fall. Individual cedars commonly grow among stands of hardwoods. The best cedars are found in water at least 5 feet deep.

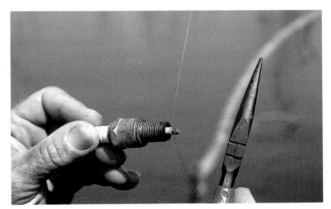

USE an old spark plug to free lures snagged in timber. With your line near vertical, pinch the electrode over the line, then drop the spark plug. If the lure doesn't come loose right away, twitch your rod tip a few times.

SLOW-ROLL a spinnerbait over brushy cover in early season. Reel just fast enough to make the blades turn, and let the lure actually bump the brush. When the lure reaches the near side of the brush, let it helicopter down.

Richland-Chambers Reservoir:

White Bass

When the "sand bass" are biting on Richland-Chambers, anglers haul them in three or four at a time. The plentiful shad crop, combined with the lake's open expanses, mean ideal conditions for white bass. The fish average about a pound, but there are a fair number in the 2- to 2½-pound range.

In late February or early March, whites begin working their way up the main creek channels. Look for them on 15- to 35-foot, clean-bottomed flats in the upper half of the lake. Fishing is usually slow in early season, but you can catch some fish by vertically jigging with a spoon or tailspin. Or, drift with a slip-sinker rig and a shiner.

By mid-March, some whites make their way into the free-flowing portions of the main creeks, miles above where you can go with a big boat. They spawn in moving water, usually along inside bends with a firm, sandy bottom and no more than 3 feet of water. Bank and small-boat fishermen catch hordes of whites by casting small jigs into the spawning areas. Most of the fish have spawned by mid-April.

After the whites finish spawning, look for them along any treelines in the upper ends of the lake. They'll often suspend from 15 to 20 feet down along fencerows, old creek beds or other distinct treelines, where you can catch them on the multiple-jig setup shown on the opposite page.

Small schools of whites also roam timbered flats along the main creek channels. The schools are tough to find and difficult to stay with if you do locate them. The best technique is casting with lures that cover a lot of water, such as vibrating plugs, minnow plugs and tailspins.

Fishing really picks up in mid-May, after the fish have moved into the big water in the lower half of the lake. Look for huge schools of whites busting shad on the surface. This pattern continues through September. Use the same lures as in post-spawn, with the addition of small propbaits, and be ready to move when the fish do. They may show up just about anywhere in the open water.

By early October, cooling temperatures push the fish to depths of 20 to 30 feet, and as the water continues to cool, they go even deeper. By mid-December, you'll find them at depths of 50 feet or more, usually near the dam.

Whites continue to feed all winter, despite the cool temperatures. Try vertically jigging with spoons or a multiple-jig setup.

Whenever you're fishing around timber, use medium-power baitcasting gear with 15- to 20-pound mono. In open water, spinning gear with 8- to 10-pound mono is sufficient.

Light showers, a gentle breeze or heavy overcast usually triggers a flurry of white bass action, especially in summer, but you can catch a few whites almost anytime. As a rule, fishing is better in morning and evening than in midday. For best surface action, fish in midweek rather than on weekends; heavy boat traffic puts the fish down.

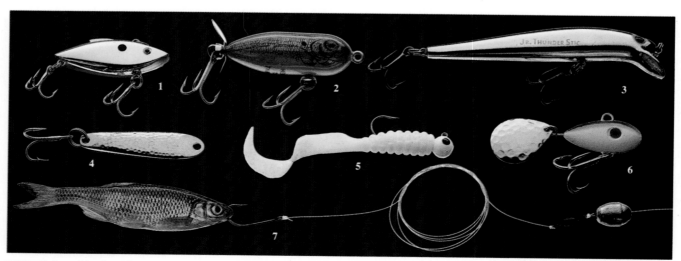

LURES for white bass include: (1) Bill Lewis Tiny Trap, a vibrating plug; (2) Heddon Tiny Torpedo, a propbait; (3) Storm Jr. Thunderstick, a floating minnow plug; (4) Hopkins Shorty, a jigging spoon; (5) Mister Twister Meeny; (6) Mann's Little George, a tailspin; (7) slip-sinker rig with 2- to 3-inch shiner and size 4 hook.

How to Catch White Bass Suspended in Timber

TIE a multiple-jig rig by threading 2 to 4 jigs, weighing 1/8-ounce each, onto 12-pound mono, then tying another jig or jigging spoon to the end of the line. Attach the jigs at 8- to 12-inch intervals using triple surgeon's knots (inset).

ANCHOR your boat by tying off to a tree. Keep your tie line short so the boat can't swing much; otherwise, you'll constantly snag up. A brush clamp comes in handy for quickly attaching a line to a limb.

LOWER the rig to an exact depth by stripping line from the reel to the first guide, which on most rods is about 2 feet. Ten strips would then get the rig down 20 feet. If nothing bites in a few minutes, try a different depth.

Crappie

When your arms get tired from hoisting 1- to 2-pound "slabs" out of the brush piles, you'll know why Richland-Chambers is rapidly gaining a reputation as one of the South's premier crappie lakes. White crappies dominate the catch, but there are plenty of blacks as well.

The action picks up in late February, when the water warms to the mid-50s and crappies begin working their way back into the creek arms. You'll find most of the fish suspended in trees alongside the creek channels, normally at depths of 12 to 20 feet. Simply tie up to a tree and lower a small jig or a split-shot rig with a minnow over the side of the boat. A medium-power spinning outfit with 12-pound mono is a good choice for this kind of fishing.

As the water continues to warm, the crappies move shallower, concentrating in brush piles in the back ends of the creek arms where the water is 4 to 6 feet deep.

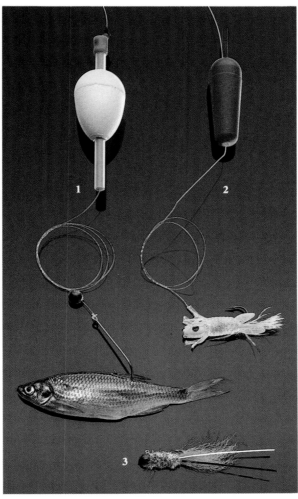

RIGS AND LURES for crappies include: (1) slip-bobber rig with size 2 Aberdeen hook and 3-inch shiner; (2) peg-bobber rig with ⅛-ounce Blue Fox Foxee Jig; (3) Original Slater's Crappie Jig. The jigs can also be tipped with a shiner.

into the brush piles. The long pole makes it easy to precisely lower your bait into small openings, and with mono of at least 12-pound test, you should be able to straighten a light-wire hook if you hang up in the branches. In narrow creeks, however, a 5- to 5½-foot spinning outfit works better than a cane or extension pole because of the tight quarters. Some anglers prefer to use a ¹⁄₁₆-ounce jig instead of a shiner, but on most days, live bait will catch more fish.

By mid-April, most of the fish have moved back to deeper parts of the creek arms. As the weather continues to warm, they work their way out of the arms, and by early June, you'll find most of them in the main lake.

Prime summer and fall crappie locations are tree lines along the edges of the main creek channels. Timber in water as deep as 45 feet will produce, with most of the fish suspended at depths of 10 to 35 feet.

You can catch crappies in these areas through November, but fishing slows considerably from mid-December through January as crappies move still deeper. It's not unusual to catch them at depths of 50 to 60 feet.

When the fish are in deep timber, snags are a constant headache. And you'll have trouble keeping hooked fish from wrapping around branches. But a "crappie stick" (p. 63) minimizes these problems.

Spawning begins in mid-March and continues into early April. Look for spawners in brushy cover at depths of 1 to 2 feet. If the creek arm is fed by a stream, the stream channel may hold crappies too. You'll find most of the fish in washouts (p. 62) and along undercut banks with exposed roots.

Use a 12- to 14-foot cane pole or extension pole to drop a bobber rig baited with a 2- to 3-inch shiner

WASHOUTS along the banks of small creeks are prime crappie spawning sites, particularly if there is submerged brush for cover.

FLOODED PECAN TREES (left) make good crappie habitat because they have many large limbs near the bottom that grow horizontally, as shown in this photo of a live pecan tree (right). Pecan trees grow as tall as 120 feet and have gnarly branches, much like those of an oak.

GRAPEVINES dangling from trees are a good summertime crappie indicator. The submerged vines make excellent crappie cover.

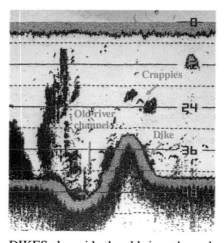

SWIRLS along the bank reveal spawning crappies. When you spot a swirl, toss a jig or minnow into the exact spot; the fish usually strikes immediately.

DEEP WATER near the dam face holds large schools of crappies in winter. Check the 40- to 55-foot depth zone; the fish hold near the bottom.

DIKES alongside the old river channel that top out at 25 to 30 feet hold crappies in summer. The dikes were originally built to prevent flooding.

How to Make and Use a "Crappie Stick"

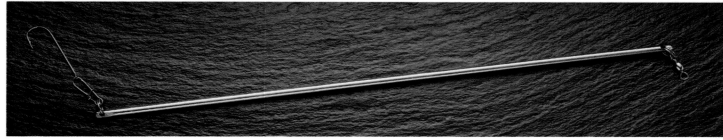

CUT a heavy metal rod into 12-inch lengths, drill holes in each end (you may have to flatten the ends first), add split rings, then attach a barrel swivel to one end and a snap with a size 1/0 Aberdeen hook to the other.

LOWER the rig vertically until you reach the desired depth. Make sure your boat is anchored securely so it doesn't swing. If you hook a limb, drop your rod tip; the weight of the crappie stick will usually free the hook.

HORSE the fish out of the cover quickly to prevent it from wrapping around a limb. The long metal rod reduces the chances that the fish will tangle in the branches, especially if you exert steady pressure.

Other Crappie-fishing Tips

USE a long-shank wire hook that will bend enough to pull free of snags. The larger the hook, the thicker the wire, and the less the hook will bend. Most anglers believe that a size 2 to 1/0 hook is ideal.

SUBSTITUTE a slip-bobber for a peg bobber if you're hanging up in shallow brush. When you get snagged, simply reel up slack and push your rod tip against the bobber, which then pushes on the split shot and hook to free the rig.

63

Richland-Chambers Reservoir:

Catfish

Richland and Chambers creeks held plenty of big cats before the dam was built, so the reservoir commonly yields catfish in the 40- to 60-pound range, despite its young age. In addition, the lake has been heavily stocked with channels and blues, most of which run from 1 to 3 pounds.

You can catch some catfish throughout the year, but they bite best at water temperatures from 55 to 80°F. When the water reaches 55, usually in early March, you'll find cats in 15 to 30 feet of water on timbered flats leading into creek arms.

The best early-season technique is chumming. Select a spot with a fairly clean bottom near an easily identifiable tree, chum it with a gallon or so of fermented grain (p. 45), then come back a few hours later. Tie up to the same tree and fish vertically with cheese-bait on a size 2 treble hook, keeping the bait a foot or two off bottom. Use a medium-heavy baitcasting outfit with 20-pound mono so you can horse the fish out of the timber.

In late May, when the water warms to the low 70s, the fish move onto brushy 2- to 7-foot flats to spawn.

Look for cormorant roosting trees; the droppings draw shad and, in turn, catfish

But they're difficult to find and don't respond to chum as well as they did before spawning time.

By mid-June, most of the fish are done spawning and are working their way toward the outer reaches of the creek arms and into the main lake, where they will stay until November. During this period you can catch them at depths of 20 to 25 feet, although some cats suspend in open water at depths of 20 feet or less. Other good summer and fall locations are stock tanks (p. 56).

Jug fishing (opposite page) works well when cats are suspended in open water. Anglers set out 8 to 15 jugs in the morning, fish for something else for a few hours, then come back to check the jugs later in the day.

By late November, the fish begin to form tighter schools, although they don't move deeper. Try chumming for them in creek channels or stock tanks.

Weather and time of day have little effect on catfish, especially when you're chumming. You can draw the fish in and start a feeding frenzy practically anytime. They seem to bite better with a light breeze, however.

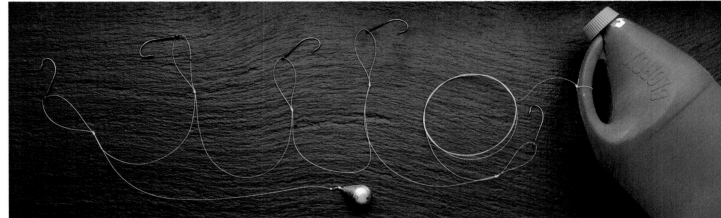

TIE 10 feet of 60-pound mono to the handle of a bleach bottle. Thread on 5 size 2/0 hooks, then add a 2- to 3-ounce weight to the other end of the line. Attach the hooks at 18-inch intervals, using the same knot as on the multiple-jig setup on p. 59. Paint the jugs fluorescent orange so you can spot them from a distance.

BAIT each hook with a minnow, crayfish, shrimp or some cheesebait, starting with the bottom hook first. Check the wind direction before setting the jugs, then place them just upwind of the area you want to fish.

CONTINUE to toss out jugs as you motor along. Spread them in a line at a right angle to the wind so each one covers different water. Finding the jugs will be easier if you set them so they drift into shore, not into open water.

USE binoculars to find the jugs. On a windy day, they may drift a mile or two, but they will usually wind up in a fairly small area.

STORE your jug lines by first dropping the weight inside. Then gather all the hooks, stuff them into the jug and screw on the cap.

Swampland Reservoirs

Despite their shallow depth, these reservoirs support a tremendous diversity of fish life

Before these reservoirs were filled, their basins were mainly swampland. And in many cases, the water level was raised less than 20 feet, so they retain their swamplike appearance.

The low-lying terrain surrounding these lakes is quite flat, with only a few subtle hills and ridges. Although a swampland reservoir's maximum depth may be 50 feet, most of the water is no deeper than 25.

As a rule, the main basins of swampland reservoirs are wide and the creek arms short – in some cases barely distinguishable from the rest of the lake.

Because the basins of these lakes contain large amounts of decaying vegetation, the water fertility is high, meaning the depths are low in oxygen in summer. Often, the water is tea-colored, the result of tannic acid produced by the decaying plants.

The warm, shallow, highly vegetated water characteristic of these lakes is ideal for largemouth bass, sunfish and crappies. In fact, the world-record white crappie (5 pounds, 3 ounces) was caught in Enid Reservoir, a swampland reservoir in Mississippi. In addition, many swampland reservoirs have good populations of chain pickerel, catfish and white bass. Some have serious roughfish problems, with an abundance of carp, which root up the bottom, and gar, which feed on young gamefish and compete with adult gamefish for food.

The low oxygen level, combined with the stained water, means that the fish live in shallow water most of the time, with the exception of late fall and winter. Then, the water mixes thoroughly, oxygenating the depths and allowing fish to go deeper.

Case Study:

Lake Bistineau, Louisiana

When you're fishing in a jungle of flooded cypress trees overgrown with Spanish moss, it's easy to see why many consider Lake Bistineau one of the most scenic bodies of water in the country.

Nearly 200 years ago, a massive logjam on the Red River flooded upstream tributaries, including Loggy Bayou, forming Lake Bistineau. Over time, however, the lake slowly drained. In 1938, the State of Louisiana built a permanent dam to preserve the water level, and in 1951, the dam was raised another 4 feet, creating the lake that exists today.

At first glance, many anglers are intimidated by the lake. It appears that navigation would be almost impossible without getting lost or hitting a submerged stump. But with a good lake map, navigation isn't too much of a problem. The main river channel and

the adjoining sloughs and bayous are well marked. Take it easy whenever you get off of a marked channel, however.

Even with a good map, it pays to carry a compass; it's easy to get disoriented in the maze of flooded cypress trees.

Channel markers show you which direction you're heading, and the numbers provide a locational reference

Lake Bistineau is unusual compared to most other man-made lakes, because its sole purpose is recreation. Besides fishing and duck hunting, the lake is used for pleasure boating and waterskiing. Bistineau has 2 public boat ramps, 2 resorts, 16 marinas and an excellent state park with rental cabins and a campground.

Best known for its largemouth bass fishing, Bistineau also produces good catches of black crappies (specks), white crappies (white perch), redear sunfish (chinquapins), yellow bass (barfish) and bluegills.

The lake also abounds with catfish, but most of them are caught on limb lines and yo-yo rigs (opposite page). Few anglers fish them with sportfishing gear.

Striped bass and hybrid stripers (wipers) have been stocked in large numbers, but the survival rate is low

Spring-loaded yo-yo rigs hook fish and pull them up

and they don't grow as large as they often do in deeper reservoirs. At present, anglers show little interest in them.

Many other species are found in the lake, but not in fishable numbers. You'll catch a few spotted bass when fishing largemouths, and warmouths and long-ear sunfish sometimes turn up when you're after bluegills or chinquapins.

The lake has an excellent population of good-sized chain pickerel (jackfish), but most local anglers consider them trash fish. Freshwater drum (goo), while regarded as trash fish in other regions, are a favorite of some anglers on Bistineau.

Seasonal warming and cooling patterns in Bistineau are the opposite of those in deeper reservoirs (p. 14). Anglers should become familiar with these patterns because they have a dramatic effect on fishing.

The reason for the difference relates to the shallow depth of the entire lakebed. With a wide, flat basin and no deep pool at the lower end, this zone warms and cools more rapidly than the upper end, where the channel is much more confined. As a result, the lower end warms about two weeks earlier than the upper end in spring, and cools about two weeks earlier in fall.

Another important difference: fishing in Lake Bistineau is affected by weather to a greater degree than in most other lakes. On a very cold night, for instance, the water temperature may drop 10 degrees, shutting down the action for most gamefish.

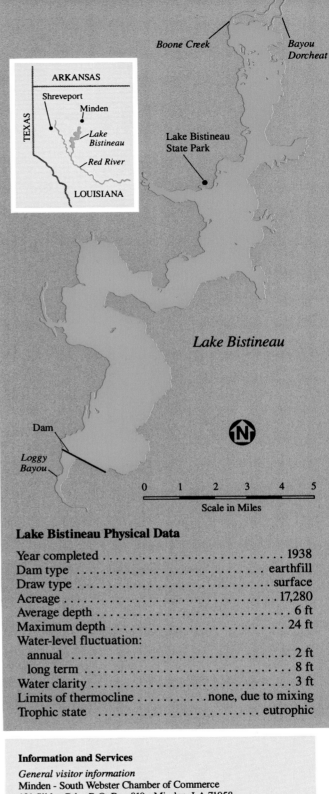

Lake Bistineau Physical Data

Year completed 1938
Dam type . . . . earthfill
Draw type . . . . surface
Acreage 17,280
Average depth . . . . 6 ft
Maximum depth . . . . 24 ft
Water-level fluctuation:
  annual . . . . 2 ft
  long term . . . . 8 ft
Water clarity . . . . 3 ft
Limits of thermocline . . . . none, due to mixing
Trophic state . . . . eutrophic

Information and Services

General visitor information
Minden - South Webster Chamber of Commerce
101 Sibley Rd. - P. O. Box 819 - Minden, LA 71058

Biologist
Louisiana Dept. of Wildlife & Fisheries
P. O. Box 915 - Minden, LA 71055

Guides
Homer Humphrey's Lake Bistineau Guide Service
702 Shirley Dr. - Minden, LA 71055

Accommodations
Lake Bistineau State Park
P. O. Box 589 - Doyline, LA 71023

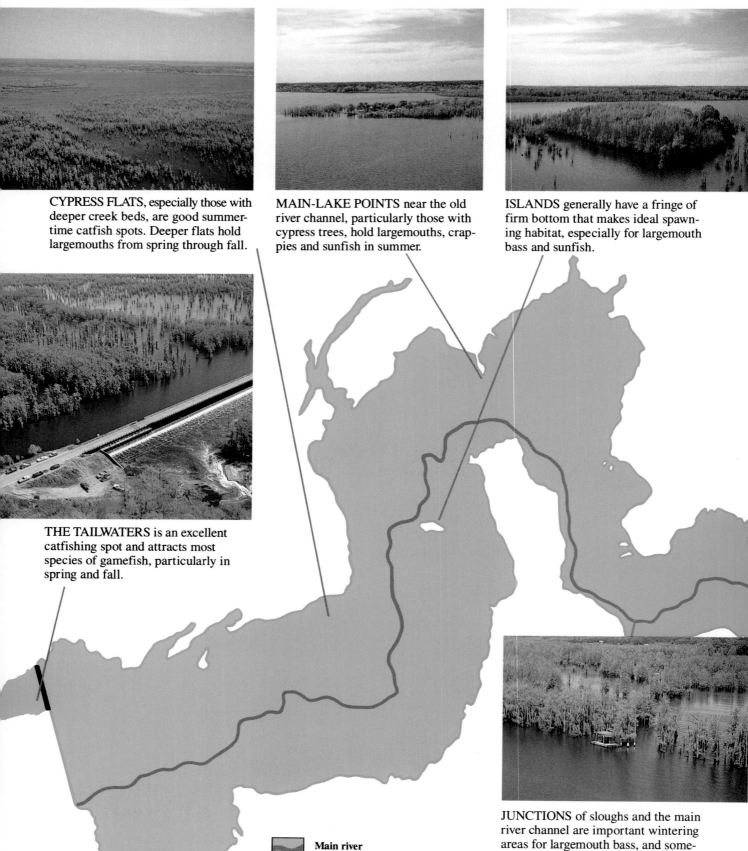

Lake Bistineau Habitat

CYPRESS FLATS, especially those with deeper creek beds, are good summertime catfish spots. Deeper flats hold largemouths from spring through fall.

MAIN-LAKE POINTS near the old river channel, particularly those with cypress trees, hold largemouths, crappies and sunfish in summer.

ISLANDS generally have a fringe of firm bottom that makes ideal spawning habitat, especially for largemouth bass and sunfish.

THE TAILWATERS is an excellent catfishing spot and attracts most species of gamefish, particularly in spring and fall.

Main river channel

JUNCTIONS of sloughs and the main river channel are important wintering areas for largemouth bass, and sometimes hold a few spotted bass.

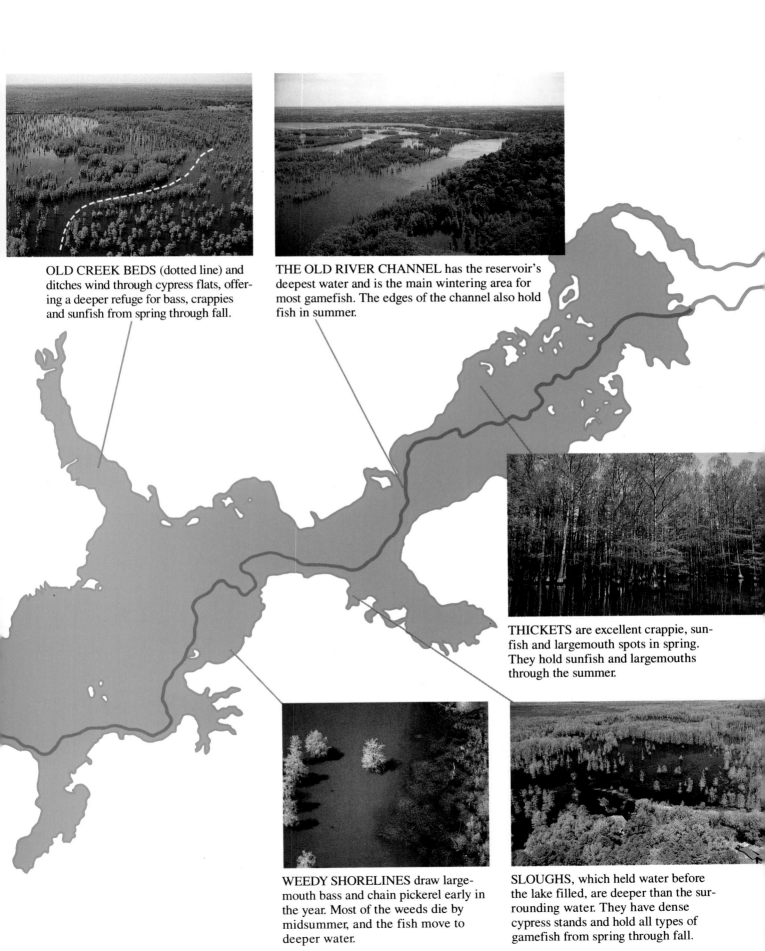

OLD CREEK BEDS (dotted line) and ditches wind through cypress flats, offering a deeper refuge for bass, crappies and sunfish from spring through fall.

THE OLD RIVER CHANNEL has the reservoir's deepest water and is the main wintering area for most gamefish. The edges of the channel also hold fish in summer.

THICKETS are excellent crappie, sunfish and largemouth spots in spring. They hold sunfish and largemouths through the summer.

WEEDY SHORELINES draw largemouth bass and chain pickerel early in the year. Most of the weeds die by midsummer, and the fish move to deeper water.

SLOUGHS, which held water before the lake filled, are deeper than the surrounding water. They have dense cypress stands and hold all types of gamefish from spring through fall.

71

Lake Bistineau:

Largemouth Bass

Tournament fishermen on Lake Bistineau know that it usually takes at least a 4-pound average to be in contention. The bass average about 3, and 7- to 8-pounders are not uncommon.

Although the bass in Bistineau move very little from season to season, they can be difficult to find in the cypress jungle. Unless you know what to look for, the trees all seem to look alike.

As a rule, trees in the vicinity of creek channels, ditches or any type of deeper channel running through the cypress flats will hold more fish than trees far up on the flats. The channels serve as migration routes and provide a deep-water refuge for fish that have been pushed out of the shallows by cold fronts or hot, still weather. Not all of these channels are obvious, so you must pay close attention to your depth finder. A break of even a foot can make a big difference.

In early March, the fish move into shallow water, usually hard-bottomed areas from 3 to 5 feet deep near shorelines or islands. But the fish are reluctant to stray far from the deeper channels.

Spawning begins in mid-March and continues into early April. Prime spawning areas include weedy flats; clean, sandy banks at depths of 2 feet or less; and cypress roots from 6 inches to 2 feet beneath the surface. Often, the fish are so shallow, you'll see their fins sticking out of the water.

To catch spawners in shallow water, try casting with a floating lizard, soft stickbait or ¼- to ⅜-ounce tandem-blade spinnerbait. Or, twitch a floating minnow plug over the beds.

After spawning, the fish slide out slightly deeper, setting up on cypress flats or in sloughs with 7- to 10-foot-deep channels. They stay in these areas until mid-November, when the water cools enough for them to move back to the same areas they used prior to spawning. They feed heavily in these areas until late December.

Once you find a cypress flat or slough, you must learn to spot the right kind of cypress trees (p. 74). If you catch a fish on a certain type of tree or tree cluster, chances are, similar trees or clusters will also produce.

The major technique for fishing the cypress is *pitchin'* (p. 75). The fish almost always hold right up against the tree, so it's extremely important to get your lure in tight. Pitchin' enables you to get your lure under the branches and set it gently in the water precisely where you want it.

A 6½- to 7-foot, medium-heavy baitcasting rod and a narrow-spool reel filled with 14- to 17-pound mono are ideal for pitchin' ⅜- to ½-ounce jigs with pork or crawworm trailers, and Texas-rigged worms, lizards, and crawworms. Pitch the lure right up to the tree or just past it, hop it 2 or 3 times, then reel in and pitch to the next target. Bistineau's cypress trees have a comparatively small root system, so you'll seldom catch a fish more than 4 feet from the tree.

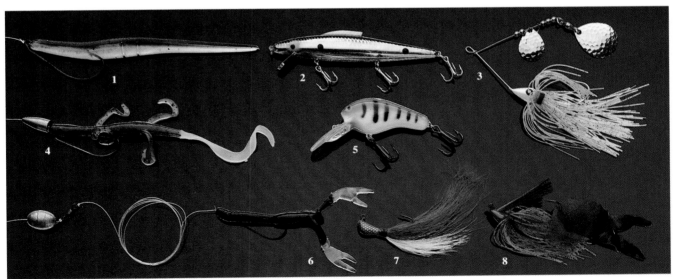

LURES for largemouth bass include: (1) Lunker City Slug-Go, a soft stickbait; (2) Bill Lewis Slap-Stick, a floating minnow plug; (3) Blue Fox Roland Martin Original Tandem Spinnerbait; (4) Toledo Tackle Lizard, Texas-rigged; (5) Sylo's Pro Lures Divin' Ace, a medium-running crankbait; (6) Stanley Hale's Craw Worm, Carolina-rigged; (7) bucktail jig; (8) Bulldog Flippin' Jig, a rubber-legged brushguard jig, with a pork trailer.

By early January, water temperatures in the low 50s drive shad and bluegills out to the main river channel, and the bass follow. You'll find them in deep, outside bends in the channel, especially around submerged brush piles. Another good wintertime spot is the junction of a slough and the main river channel.

The fish are sluggish in winter, but you can often catch them on a Carolina-rigged lizard. Rigged this way, the lizard sinks slowly, tempting the fish to bite.

Another good wintertime lure is a ⅜- to ½-ounce jig with a large pork trailer. As a rule, a jig will catch fewer, but larger, fish.

Late-winter and early-spring rains increase the river's flow, often causing it to rise 3 or 4 feet. You'll find bass along the downstream edges of sandbars in the main channel.

Where the current flows over the adjacent flats, look for the fish in channels running perpendicular to the current or in eddies that form behind large trees.

Anchor downstream of the spot you want to fish, cast upstream with a ¼-ounce bucktail jig and work it back slowly. This unusual technique produces some impressive catches under what most anglers consider to be adverse conditions.

How to Spot Productive Cypress Trees

POINT TREES. Active bass usually hold on the outside edge of the outermost trees in a cluster. When the fish are not active, they're usually found in pockets between the trees (below).

THICKETS. Dense clusters of trees in shallow water hold lots of minnows and sunfish, so they attract pre-spawn bass. Deeper thickets provide food and shade for bass during the summer.

EXPOSED ROOTS. Visible roots alongside cypress trees indicate mats of submerged roots. Bass are more likely to hold around trees with heavy root growth than around slick trees.

POCKETS. Trees growing in a ring form a pocket that often holds bass. If a pocket has submerged roots extending across it, like the exposed roots in the inset, it makes a good nesting site.

"GRANDDADDY" CYPRESS TREES. Huge trees in deep sloughs often hold bass in summer because the massive root systems offer more shade than those of smaller trees.

74

How to Pitch in the Cypress

PULL out enough line so the lure reaches back to the reel. Start the pitchin' motion with the reel at chest level and hold the rod at the 4 o'clock position. Keep the reel in free-spool and the spool tension loose.

SWEEP the rod forward, pulling the lure out of your hand. Stop the sweep at 2 o'clock so the lure maintains a low trajectory. If you bring the rod up too much, the lure will travel in a high arc and catch limbs.

STOP the lure in the precise spot by thumbing it *before* it touches down. The lure should enter the water with practically no splash. With the spool tension loose, the reel will backlash if you don't thumb it.

Tips for Catching Largemouths

TIP your jig with a larger pork chunk to slow the sink rate. Largemouths often hang beneath shallow cypress limbs. If the jig sinks too fast, they may ignore it or miss it.

LOOK for schools of bass around cypress tree points along the main river channel in summer. Sometimes these spots hold a dozen or more 2- to 5-pound bass.

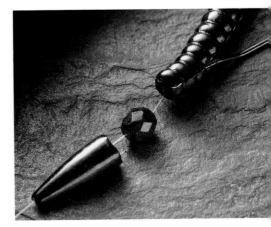

ADD a glass bead between your worm sinker and hook. The noise made by the sinker clicking against the bead helps attract largemouth bass in the dark-colored water.

Lake Bistineau:
Crappie

When the "specks" are hitting on Lake Bistineau, it's not unusual to catch a basketful averaging more than a pound, and there's a chance for one over 3.

Specks (black crappie) outnumber "white perch" (white crappie), although there are good numbers of them as well.

In mid-March, crappies move into 3- to 5-foot-deep cypress thickets to spawn; they deposit their eggs at water temperatures in the low 60s. But it's tough to find a concentration at spawning time. You'll catch a fish or two around a particular tree, then you'll have to work several other trees to find more fish.

LURES for crappies include: (1) Wazp Flashaboo Jig on slip-bobber rig, (2) ball-head jig tipped with shiner on peg-bobber rig, (3) Wazp Feather Jig.

Most of the crappies have completed spawning by mid-April and are moving to deeper water. Look for them at depths of 8 to 12 feet, in or near sloughs, deep creek channels or the main river channel.

Local anglers have placed thousands of brush piles, or "tops," along the fringes of the channels, and that's where the majority of crappies are caught through the summer. But you can also catch them around natural brush piles, such as blown-down cypress trees. The fish stay in these spots until mid-November.

Even if you don't know where the tops are, you should be able to find some if you spend a little time graphing the channel edges.

Once you find a likely-looking top, anchor your boat in a position so you can easily reach it. The best way to fish the tops is by tightlining. Using a 12-foot graphite extension pole and 6-pound mono, lower a $\frac{1}{32}$-ounce hair or feather jig and fish it vertically, bouncing the jig over the tops and into pockets in the brush. Some anglers like to tip their jigs with $1\frac{1}{2}$-inch shiner minnows; others fish them plain.

If you're having trouble snagging up in the tops, add a small float to keep the jig riding just above the brush. You sacrifice a little feel this way, however.

You can also use a light spinning outfit and a jig or minnow fished beneath a slip-bobber. Or, use spinning gear to bounce $\frac{1}{16}$- to $\frac{1}{8}$-ounce brushguard jigs (below) over the tops. Always use light monofilament, 4- to 6-pound test; heavy line restricts the action of your jig.

By late November, cooling water has driven crappies into holes at least 15 feet deep in the main river channel. But they're still relating to brushy cover, such as fallen trees and brush piles.

The best way to find crappies in winter is to cruise the main channel with a graph. The fish are often suspended in tight schools, and locating them is difficult without good electronics. When you find a school, get ready for some fast action and the biggest fish of the year. Tightlining is the primary wintertime technique.

Crappies generally bite best in the morning. Fishing is slow in midday, and picks up a little toward evening. Night fishing is poor because of the dark water.

Overcast skies cause crappies to suspend farther above the brush tops. On calm, sunny days, they tend to bury in the brush where it's difficult to get a bait to them.

Tips for Catching Crappies

DABBLE a small jig in the tops using a graphite extension pole. These ultrasensitive poles make it possible to feel the twigs so you can drop your jig into pockets in the brush. And you can easily feel even the lightest bite.

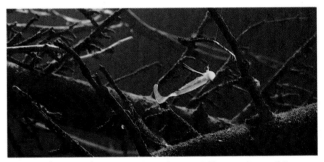

USE a $\frac{1}{16}$- to $\frac{1}{8}$-ounce brushguard jig, such as this Northland Weed-Less Sink'n jig head, when fishing in heavy brush. A brushguard will prevent most snags, but if you do hang up, free the jig as shown below.

UNSNAG jigs using a 1-ounce bell sinker with a snap attached to it (inset). Simply clip the sinker onto your line and drop it. If it doesn't free the jig immediately, jiggle the rod a little so the sinker bounces on the jig.

Lake Bistineau:

Sunfish

As soon as the "chinquapins" start bedding in Lake Bistineau, the word spreads fast. Everyone knows that the spawning period is the best time to get the big redears – fish running from ½ to 1½ pounds. The lake also holds good numbers of bluegills in the ½-pound class.

A few weeks before spawning, usually mid-March, sunfish show up in dense cypress thickets where the water is 3 to 4 feet deep. But they don't bed in these areas because they're too shady. Most spawning takes place on open, sandy-bottomed flats at depths of 1 to 5 feet, often around clumps of buttonbush or big cypress stumps.

In a normal year, the good-sized chinquapins start to bed about the second week in April. When you find a bed, you can often catch several dozen fish. Carefully note the location of good beds; they'll be in the same place next year. Spawning continues for 3 to 4

weeks, then the fish scatter into deeper water and are difficult to find.

The bluegills move in to spawn about the time the chinquapins are starting to move out, usually in early May. Often the two use the same nests. You can find bluegills on the beds until late June. They leave the beds when hot weather sets in.

Bluegills start bedding again in August, but not in the same spots they used earlier. Late summer beds are usually in 5 to 6 feet of water adjacent to the main river channel. Bedding continues well into September.

The best bait for chinquapins is 1½-inch crayfish. Local anglers often dip-net them out of road ditches (opposite page), but you can buy them at most bait shops. For bluegills, it's hard to beat a small catalpa worm, a cricket or Eurolarvae. Earthworms also work well, for both species.

Dangle the bait beneath a small float with only a split shot for weight. Most anglers use 12-foot extension poles, but some prefer light spinning outfits. You'll get more bites with light mono, no more than 6-pound test.

Sunfish in Lake Bistineau generally bite best in late afternoon and early evening. The action is fastest under cloudy, rather than sunny, skies.

BAITS for sunfish include: (1) red wiggler; (2) 1- to 2-inch crayfish; (3) cricket; and (4) small catalpa worm, all on size 6 or 8 long-shank Aberdeen hooks. You can also use (5) Eurolarvae on an ice fly.

Tips for Finding and Catching Sunfish

LOOK for clumps of buttonbush; they're good indicators of sunfish spawning sites. The bushes grow only on a hard, sandy bottom, the same kind sunfish use for nesting.

SCOUT for beds by slipping along slowly with an electric motor, continually tossing your bobber rig ahead of the boat. When you get a bite, stop and fish the area thoroughly.

DIP-NET small crayfish out of road ditches that have permanent standing water (left). Look for areas with a gravelly or rocky bottom. Using a long-handled net with mesh no larger than ¼ inch, simply scoop along the bottom. If you find the right kind of area, you may get a dozen or two crayfish in a single dip (right). The best size for bait is about 1½ inches.

KEEP crickets in a container that dispenses them one at a time. This model snaps shut after you shake out a cricket. Keep the dispenser in a cool spot, out of the sun.

Lake Bistineau:
Other Species

A smorgasbord of fish species inhabit Lake Bistineau. In addition to the gamefish discussed earlier in the case study, there are three species of catfish (channel, flathead and blue) and three species of temperate bass (striped, white and yellow), as well as the wiper (opposite page). You'll also find a few spotted bass and longear sunfish, and even some chain pickerel.

BLUE CATFISH, called "high fins" (shown), and channel catfish are usually caught on trotlines and limblines. They run 3 to 8 pounds. Anglers catch a few on cheesebait, bloodbait, shrimp, crayfish and cutbait.

FLATHEAD CATFISH, known locally as "Appaluchions" or "opps," are most often caught on limblines baited with small sunfish. Opps normally range from 5 to 15 pounds, but there's a chance for fish up to 60.

SPOTTED BASS are sometimes caught on sandy points along the main river channel in the upper end of the lake; they're normally deeper than large-mouths. They run 1 to 2 pounds, with an occasional fish up to 3.

YELLOW BASS, called "barfish" or "sharks," grow large in Bistineau, some-times exceeding a pound. They're easiest to catch in spring, when they swim upstream to spawn on shallow sandbars in the main river.

WIPERS are produced in hatcheries by crossing female striped bass with male white bass. They're caught in the upper river in spring and in open water of the main lake in summer. They run 1 to 3 pounds.

LONGEAR SUNFISH, called "strawberry bream," thrive in the river above the lake, but some are caught in the lake proper. Smaller than bluegills or redears, longears seldom exceed 6 ounces. They're easily identified by the long, black earflap with a light-colored margin.

CHAIN PICKEREL, or "jackfish," are often caught by largemouth bass fishermen. Pickerel run good-sized, from 2 to 3 pounds.

Eastern Mountain Reservoirs

These deep, clear lakes offer superb multispecies fishing

S ometimes called *hill-land*, *highland* or *cove reservoirs*, these deep, steep-sided lakes are found in hilly or mountainous terrain, mainly in the eastern half of the country. The long, narrow basins exceed 100 feet in depth, and the creek arms (coves) may be several miles long.

Most of these lakes were made for the main purposes of power generation, flood control and navigation, so water levels vary greatly throughout the year. The

level is gradually drawn down over the summer, sometimes by 50 feet or more, providing water to generate power and maintain downstream flows and, at the same time, making room for spring runoff.

These drastic water-level fluctuations limit growth of aquatic vegetation. Plants that took root at high water are exposed when the water drops, and those that took root at low water do not get enough sunlight when the water rises. Besides rocks, the main

types of cover are flooded timber and brush, which may also be in short supply because many of these basins were clear-cut before being filled.

Water fluctuations may also inhibit fish spawning. Any change in water level around spawning time reduces hatching success.

Although these lakes are normally very clear, spring runoff may color the water, especially in the upper end of the lake and in arms fed by good-sized creeks. Fertility levels in most mountain lakes are quite low, so the depths stay well-oxygenated throughout the year.

White bass and black bass, including largemouth, smallmouth and sometimes spotted, are native to most of these lakes. Striped bass or hybrids (white x striped bass) have been stocked in many mountain reservoirs. These species thrive because of the plenti-

ful supply of shad. Crappies and sunfish inhabit secondary and tertiary (p. 8) creek arms, but the scarcity of woody cover limits their numbers.

Walleyes inhabited many mountain rivers and streams before they were dammed, but the native fish have now disappeared from most of the lakes and stocking is necessary to maintain walleye populations.

Mountain reservoirs with enough cold, well-oxygenated water in the depths are sometimes stocked with trout, primarily rainbows and browns.

The world's biggest walleyes and smallmouth bass are caught in mountain reservoirs. Greer's Ferry Lake, Arkansas, for instance, has produced several walleyes over 20 pounds. And the world-record smallmouth, 11 pounds, 15 ounces, was taken in Dale Hollow Reservoir, on the Kentucky-Tennessee border, in 1955.

Case Study:

Lake Cumberland, Kentucky

Sprawling through the Cumberland foothills of the Appalachians, this deep, cold mountain lake was created in 1950, when the U.S. Army Corps of Engineers completed the Wolf Creek Dam across the Cumberland River. The reservoir reduces flooding and the discharge generates enough power for a city of 375,000.

Like most mountain lakes, Cumberland has a deep, steep-sided basin and clear, infertile water. The depths stay cold and well-oxygenated all year. The main lake, which is 101 miles long, is only one mile across at its widest point. The main creek arms are 10 to 15 miles long, with many secondary and tertiary arms.

Although the lake has plenty of rocky points, bluff faces, humps and ledges, other types of natural fish cover are scarce. The entire lake basin was cleared of timber before the lake was flooded, and because the water level fluctuates as much as 50 feet over the year, there is little aquatic vegetation. However, the Kentucky Department of Fish and Wildlife Resources has placed hundreds of brush piles throughout the lake, and trees slide into the water as the bluffs erode or are cut intentionally by anglers.

As in most deep, cold reservoirs, the upper end of Lake Cumberland warms up earlier than the lower end. In most years, the difference is a week to 10 days. The upper end also tends to be murkier.

Although Lake Cumberland now boasts one of the country's premier striper fisheries, an equally good walleye fishery vanished when the Cumberland River was impounded.

In years past, the Cumberland River system was famous for its giant walleyes. Besides the 25-pound world record caught in Old Hickory Lake in 1960, the Kentucky record, a 21-pound, 8-ouncer, was taken in Lake Cumberland in 1958.

But the native Cumberland River walleyes were a river-spawning strain and, after the river was impounded, they gradually disappeared. Lake Cumberland was then restocked with the Lake Erie strain of walleyes, which are lake spawners, but do not grow as large.

Cumberland also has excellent fisheries for largemouth, smallmouth and spotted bass. Because the Wolf Creek Dam has a coldwater discharge, the river downstream of the reservoir stays cold enough for trout for a distance of 85 miles. Browns and rainbows are stocked annually, with many of the browns reaching trophy size.

Crappies (black and white) and sunfish (bluegill and longear) abound in Lake Cumberland, but they're on the small side. Other common species of gamefish include channel and flathead catfish, white bass and sauger.

Special regulations have been established to promote quality fishing in Lake Cumberland. The current limit on stripers is 3 per day, and there is a 15-inch minimum size limit on largemouths, smallmouths and walleyes.

Like most southern reservoirs, Cumberland has a healthy forage crop consisting mainly of threadfin and gizzard shad, in addition to plenty of crayfish and small sunfish. There's also a booming population of skipjack herring, an open-water forage fish that makes excellent striper food.

Besides fishing, the reservoir also supplies other forms of water-based recreation, such as swimming, waterskiing, pleasure boating and scuba diving. There are 11 privately owned marinas, 11 public boat ramps, 3 state parks with campgrounds and 16 private campgrounds.

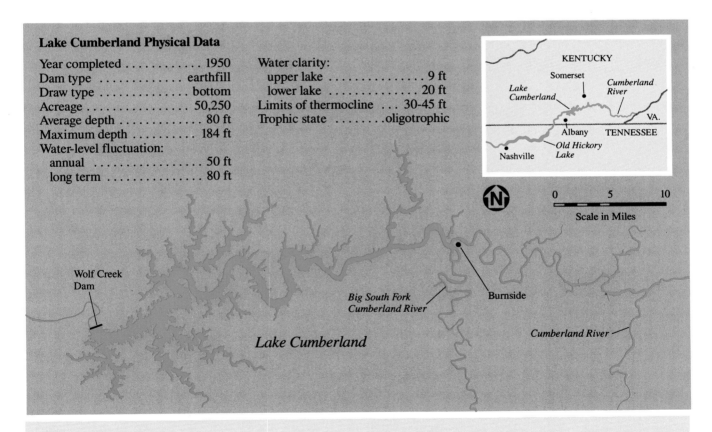

Lake Cumberland Physical Data

Year completed 1950	Water clarity:
Dam type . . . . earthfill	upper lake . . . . 9 ft
Draw type . . . . bottom	lower lake . . . . 20 ft
Acreage 50,250	Limits of thermocline . . . 30-45 ft
Average depth . . . . 80 ft	Trophic state . . . . oligotrophic
Maximum depth . . . . 184 ft	
Water-level fluctuation:	
annual . . . . 50 ft	
long term . . . . 80 ft	

KENTUCKY
Somerset
Lake Cumberland
Cumberland River
VA.
Albany TENNESSEE
Old Hickory Lake
Nashville

0   5   10
Scale in Miles

Wolf Creek Dam

Big South Fork Cumberland River

Burnside

Lake Cumberland

Cumberland River

Information and Services

General visitor information
Resource Manager - Lake Cumberland
1000 Boat Dock Road - Somerset, KY 42501

Accommodations
Grider Hill Dock
Rt. 4 - Box 800 - Albany KY 42602

Guides
Fish Tales Guide Service
(Tony Campisano, Randall Gibson, Brian Sasser)
8605 Shelbyville Road - Unit 201
Louisville, KY 40222

Biologist
Kentucky Dept. of Fish & Wildlife Resources
2073 N. Hwy. 25-W
Williamsburg, KY 40769

STEEP ROCKY BLUFFS make good year-round habitat for spotted bass and hold smallmouths in summer. The best bluffs have fallen trees for cover.

ROCKY POINTS with a gradual taper are top smallmouth areas from summer through winter. They're also good for summertime spots and largemouths.

SECONDARY CREEK ARMS are prime spawning areas for all black bass. Smaller tertiary arms also draw bass and sunfish at spawning time.

THE POOL AREA above the dam holds stripers all year. The riprapped shorelines draw smallmouths in summer and fall and walleyes year-round.

ROCK SLIDES may provide the only cover along steep bluffs. They hold walleyes, smallmouths, spots and stripers from summer through winter.

BRUSHY FLATS in shallow creek arms are excellent early-season largemouth spots. They also attract bluegills from spring through fall.

FALLEN TREES, intentionally cut for fish cover, draw largemouths and sunfish from spring through fall. They're best when the leaves are still green.

Main river channel

MAIN CREEK ARMS draw spawning stripers in spring. Largemouth, smallmouth and spotted bass can be found around points in the arms in summer.

MAIN-LAKE POINTS, especially those with timbered lips, hold largemouth, smallmouth and spotted bass from spring through fall and stripers in early spring.

BROKEN-ROCK BANKS with soft clay produce a mudline when the wind blows in, attracting walleyes and smallmouths from spring through fall.

Lake Cumberland:
Striped Bass

Veteran Lake Cumberland guides believe the next world-record striper may well be lurking in the lake's chilly depths. Cumberland has everything a striper needs to reach trophy size: cool, well-oxygenated water and an ample supply of food in the abundant shad and skipjack herring crop.

Twenty- to 30-pounders are routine during the peak fishing months and several 40-pounders are taken each season. The lake has even produced a few 50s, including the current Kentucky record, a 58-pound, 4-ouncer.

In January, stripers begin working their way up creek arms. Biologists call this migration a mock spawning run, because the fish cannot spawn successfully in the lake environment. The main wintertime technique is multi-line trolling with live baitfish, mainly shad and suckers, at depths of 30 to 60 feet. Cumberland trollers use the same technique as trollers on Elephant Butte (p. 43). But on Cumberland, side planers (p. 91) are often added to cover a wider swath of water.

You can also catch stripers in winter by vertically jigging with spoons or bucktail jigs. Make long upward sweeps of your rod to lift the lure 5 or 6 feet, then quickly lower the rod. The fish usually strike when the lure is sinking.

By early April, most stripers have reached the upper ends of the creek arms, where they will attempt to spawn. You can find some fish throughout the arms, but the heaviest striper concentrations will be around points in the upper halves, generally at depths of 20 feet or less.

The most effective springtime technique is casting a floating minnow plug or large chugger on a calm day. Work minnow plugs slowly enough so they stay near the surface and make a heavy wake; jerk chuggers hard, for maximum splash (p. 90-91). Spoons, spinners and bucktail jigs tipped with plastic curlytails also work well, as does slow-trolling with live baitfish. These techniques will take fish in the upper parts of the creek arms through May.

LURES for stripers include: (1) Cordell Pencil Popper, a chugger; (2) Blue Fox Super Vibrax spinner; (3) Cordell Redfin, a floating minnow plug; (4) Luhr-Jensen Crippled Herring, a jigging spoon; (5) live shad on trailer-hook rig with size 2/0 chemically sharpened hooks; (6) bucktail jig tipped with curlytail.

Jump-fishing for Stripers

LOOK for schools of stripers chasing shad on the surface. When you spot fish in the "jumps," motor to within 100 yards or so, then put down your trolling motor and sneak quietly to within casting distance.

CAST well past the surfacing fish, using a large floating minnow plug. If possible, position your boat so it is upwind of the school. This way, you can use the wind to your advantage for longer casts.

RETRIEVE the minnow plug just fast enough so its back is barely out of the water, creating a noticeable wake. If you reel too fast, the plug will dive beneath the surface, and the fish will usually ignore it.

In spring, you'll often see schools of stripers busting shad on the surface in morning and evening. But if you run your outboard up to the school and start casting, you'll spook them. Instead, sneak up with your trolling motor.

Although April and May are prime striper months, June and July are even better. The fish have completed their mock spawn and are gorging themselves on shad as they gradually work their way back down the creek arms. You'll still catch surface-feeding stripers by casting minnow plugs or chuggers in morning and evening. But the fish go as deep as 35 feet in midday, so you'll have to slow-troll with live bait or vertically jig with a jigging spoon or bucktail jig.

By early August, you'll find most of the stripers in the main lake, usually at depths of 35 to 60 feet, although a few remain in the mouths of major creek arms. Use a graph to scout for stripers or schools of shad along deep ledges or sharp drops near the old river channel. If you find shad, the stripers will usually be 5 to 20 feet beneath them. Slow-trolling with live bait and vertical jigging continue to produce, but the fish may be scattered. Some anglers prefer to troll jigs and minnow plugs on downriggers so they can cover more water.

Beginning in early November, stripers return to the mouths of creek arms, where they'll stay until January, when they begin to feel the spawning urge.

Wintertime fishing may be slow, especially when the water temperature dips below 50°F, but you can catch some fish by slow-trolling live baitfish or still-fishing cutbait on a gravel bottom at depths of 20 to 25 feet. Rig the bait as shown on the opposite page, cast it out, put your rod in a rod holder and wait for a bite.

Stripers roam open water in pursuit of food; the spot where you find them one day may be devoid of fish the next. If you're not sure where to look, start near the dam. The deep water above the dam is a prime wintertime striper area, but it holds some fish all year.

As a rule, stripers bite best very early or very late in the day. The bite extends later into the day in overcast weather than in calm, sunny weather. Prior to spawning, stripers feed heavily after dark, and sometimes through the night. Night fishing is usually best 2 or 3 days either side of the full moon.

A good all-purpose striper outfit consists of a 7-foot, medium-heavy baitcasting rod or flippin' stick and a heavy-duty reel with 17- to 20-pound mono. With a quality graph, you can see stripers or schools of shad, which indicate that you're in the right area and help you find the best depth. You'll need a large, aerated and insulated bait tank to keep baitfish alive, particularly in hot weather.

How to Use a Side-planer for Multi-line Trolling

ATTACH a rubber-jawed alligator clip with a split ring to replace the plastic clip, which could damage your line.

REPLACE the snap at the rear of the planer with a snap-swivel so the fish can't twist your line should it roll.

CAREFULLY BEND the metal bar on the planer slightly downward. This way, it will plane farther to the side.

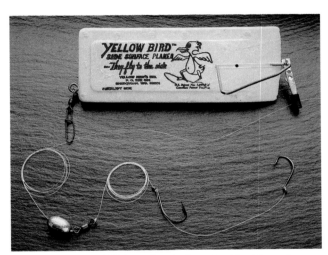

SPLICE in a size 3/0 barrel swivel, and add a ½- to 1-ounce sinker and size 2/0 hook with a 2/0 trailer. Let out the desired amount of line, then attach the snap and clip.

FEED line as the planer pulls to the side; it will go out as far as 50 feet. When a fish strikes, the alligator clip will detach, and the planer will slide down to the sinker.

Striper-fishing Tips

MAKE a cutbait rig by slicing just behind the gill of a shad, sucker or bluegill, and rigging it on a size 3/0 to 5/0 hook with a 2-foot leader and a ½- to 1-ounce egg sinker.

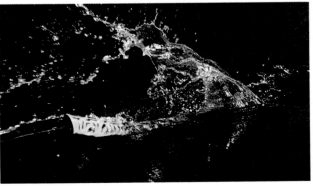

JERK a large chugger hard enough to produce violent splashes. The surface commotion attracts stripers; they probably mistake the splashing for other stripers busting shad.

Lake Cumberland:

Largemouth Bass

A look at the old "braggin' boards" around Lake Cumberland shows that largemouth fishing during the lake's boom cycle in the 50s and 60s was incredible by today's standards. Stringers of 5- to 8-pounders were commonplace, with some as large as 11. You can still catch trophy bass, but the percentage of big ones is much lower.

Largemouths turn on in March, as warming water draws them into the upper ends of creek arms. As a rule, you'll find them farther up the arms than spotted or small-mouth bass.

Most tertiary and some secondary creek arms with shallow, discolored water and brushy cover will attract largemouths after a few warm spring days in a row. You'll find them at depths of 5 to 15 feet, often around submerged treetops. On sunny days, they often hold on steep shale banks, where the water is slightly warmer. Don't hesitate to fish under mats of floating debris and pollen, which provide good overhead cover.

The best way to fish tight pockets in the brush and to penetrate the mats of debris is flippin' (p. 37) with a 3/8-ounce jig-and-pig. Other good pre-spawn patterns are twitch-ing floating minnow plugs on the surface, or bulging spinnerbaits along creek arm banks leading into spawning areas.

The fish normally start bedding in mid-April, when the water tem-perature reaches the mid-60s. They build their nests at depths of 1 to 4 feet, usually on gradually sloping banks with a gravel bottom, and often beneath overhanging tree limbs. Seldom do they spawn where a creek flows in.

LURES include: (1) Hart Beater, a buzzbait; (2) Bulldog Hawg Dawg Spinnerbait with craw-frog trailer; (3) Smithwick Rogue, a floating minnow plug; (4) Rebel Pop-R, a chugger; (5) Hopkin's Smoothie, a jigging spoon; (6) Poe's Super Cedar series 400, a deep-diving crankbait; (7) Penetrator Jig, a rubber-legged brush-guard jig with pork trailer; (8) Lunker City Slug-Go, a soft stickbait; (9) Johnson Super Floater Worm; (10) Original Culprit, a Texas-rigged ribbontail worm.

If you can see largemouths on the beds, try twitching a floating worm or minnow plug right over them. You may have to skip the worm under limbs to reach the fish (below).

Bass throughout most of the lake complete spawning by mid-May. As the water warms into the 70s, they move farther down the creek arms, holding at depths of 8 to 20 feet on shoreline points and sharp breaks along the creek channels, especially where you find brush or stumps. Or, they may suspend just off these areas. Work the heavy cover and open water adjacent to it with soft stickbaits or topwaters, using medium-power spinning or baitcasting gear and 10-pound mono.

In early July, largemouths start moving deeper. Look for them on major points in the creek arms or the main lake, generally at depths of 25 to 45 feet. Rounded points with stumps generally hold the most fish. At times, you'll find largemouths suspended off points or bluffs. Summertime fishing can be tough because of heavy boat traffic, especially on weekends, so many anglers prefer night fishing. After dark, the fish move up to depths of 15 to 20 feet on the points. Work these areas with a plastic worm, Texas-rigged with a ¼- to ⅜-ounce bullet sinker, a jig-and-pig or a ⅜-ounce single-blade spinnerbait. To slow the sink rate and interest bigger bass, try tipping your spinnerbait with a pork chunk.

The summer pattern usually holds until mid-September. Then, largemouths move back up the creek arms and begin feeding more heavily. By early October, you'll find them at the upper ends of major creek arms, especially around downed trees, brush, broken ledge rock, boulders or indentations in the bank. Work water less than 15 feet deep with topwaters, such as buzzbaits and chuggers, or try bulging spinnerbaits on the surface. Morning and evening surface action continues until the water temperature drops to 55°F, normally in late November.

When the fish aren't feeding on the surface, try crankbaiting 15- to 25-foot flats adjacent to the creek channels with a deep-diving shad imitation.

As the water continues to cool, bass suspend at depths of 15 to 25 feet over creek channels from 30 to 60 feet deep, or they move into the main lake and suspend off major points. These suspended fish are tough to catch, but you can take a few by working the edges of the structure with a ¼- to ⅜-ounce jig-and-pig or by jigging a ¼- to ⅜-ounce spoon just off the breakline.

The best time to catch wintertime bass is a day or two after a heavy rain. Warmer, darker water flowing into the head of a creek arm draws bass into 5 to 15 feet of water and turns them on. As long as the water stays warmer than normal, a crankbait or spinnerbait retrieved along the mudline is an effective presentation.

Because the trees were cleared before the lake filled, there's usually no need for heavy tackle. Most anglers prefer spinning gear with 8- to 10-pound mono or a baitcasting outfit with 10- to 14-pound mono, all medium power. For flippin' in heavy brush, however, use a stiff flippin' stick with 25-pound mono.

In Cumberland's clear water, largemouths generally bite best early and late in the day, or whenever the light is low. But from late fall through early spring, the action is fastest on sunny afternoons, when the water is warmest.

How to Fish a Floating Worm

SKIP an unweighted, Texas-rigged worm under the cover, using a 6½-foot, fast-tip spinning outfit and 10-pound mono. Use a bulky worm because it has more surface area, making it easier to skip than a thin-bodied worm.

TWITCH the worm on a slack line, making it dart sideways while moving only slightly forward. Continue to twitch and hesitate, trying to keep the worm under the cover. If you jerk the worm on a taut line, it will just move forward.

WATCH closely when a fish bites; often it will grab the worm by the tail. Wait until the fish has the head of the worm in its mouth before attempting to set the hook. This strategy will greatly improve your hooking percentage.

Lake Cumberland:
Spotted Bass

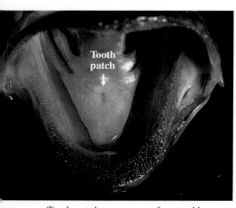

Tooth patch on tongue of spotted bass

What Cumberland's spots lack in size, they make up for in numbers. Although most of them run less than a pound, there's a chance to catch one over 5.

At first glance, spots look like largemouths, but they have wider blotches on the side and a small patch of teeth on their tongue (left). Their lower jaw does not extend past the eye, as it does on the largemouth.

As the water starts to warm in spring, spots move into coves off the main creek arms, especially those with plenty of brush and fallen trees. Toss a ¼-ounce willowleaf spinnerbait past the cover and retrieve right through it, keeping your rod tip high so the lure bulges the surface.

This technique produces until the fish start to spawn, which is normally about early to mid-April, a little before largemouths. They also build their nests in slightly deeper water, usually from 2 to 5 feet. and not as far back in the creeks. Often, they nest on shale ledges in pockets off the creek arms. Some fish spawn on points in the creek arms and main lake.

When you see spotted bass nesting, toss a small stickbait or floating minnow plug past the bed and retrieve so it runs directly over the fish. Work a stickbait with a slow, walk-the-dog retrieve; a minnow plug, with a twitch-and-pause retrieve. Another good

Tips for Finding Spotted Bass

STEEP ROCK LEDGES hold spots all year. They spend much of their time suspended in open water off the ledges, moving onto the ledges to feed on crayfish and baitfish.

OVERHEAD COVER, such as branches or horizontal rock overhangs along an otherwise clean ledge, is a magnet for spotted bass. Such cover will almost always hold a fish or two.

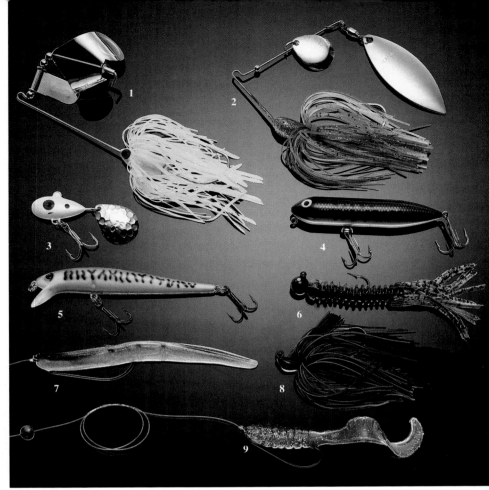

LURES include: (1) Mann's Classic Buzz Bait; (2) Stanley Vibra-Shaft Spinnerbait; (3) Mann's Little George, a tailspin; (4) Heddon Zara Puppy, a stickbait; (5) Storm Jr. Thunderstick, a floating minnow plug; (6) ball-head jig with soft-plastic ringworm; (7) Lunker City Slug-Go, a soft stickbait; (8) Stanley Jig, a rubber-legged brushguard jig with pork trailer; (9) Ditto Baby Fat Grub on split-shot rig.

technique for enticing spawners is twitching soft stickbaits (p. 97). Spotted bass continue spawning through late May.

Many fish that spawned in the creek arms return to the main lake after spawning, but some stay in the creek arms all year, dropping a little farther down toward the mouth. Use the same methods as in the pre-spawn and spawning periods, or try working a ¼-ounce jig-and-pig along steep shale banks and off rocky main-lake points.

Spotted bass can be difficult to catch in summer, because of their tendency to go very deep and suspend. By mid-June, it's not unusual to find them at depths of 45 to 60 feet, particularly off steep rocky points in the creek arms and on long main-lake points and deep reefs. Large spots are usually found in deeper water than small ones.

When spots are suspended, try fishing them at night or on cloudy days. Then, they move up to depths of 15 to 25 feet and hold tighter to structure, so they're easier to find and more aggressive.

The trick to finding summertime spots is to look for schools of shad; spots will probably be at the same depth. Productive techniques include counting down ¼- to ⅜-ounce tailspins and jigs tipped with soft-plastic grubs, and finesse fishing (p. 39) weenie worms and grubs.

In September, spots that were suspended in deep water begin to suspend closer to the surface, often only 20 feet down. They'll come up to strike a ¼- to ⅜-ounce spinnerbait bulged on the surface, or a ¼-ounce single-blade buzzbait. This pattern holds up through November.

Like largemouths, spots move into the warmer, darker water at the back ends of active creek arms following a heavy winter rain. A ¼-ounce tandem-blade willowleaf spinnerbait retrieved along the mud-line is an excellent lure choice.

Because Lake Cumberland has very little submerged timber or brush, you can use the same lighter-than-normal tackle for spotted bass as you would for smallmouths (p. 97).

LURES AND BAITS for smallmouths include: (1) Stanley Vibra-Shaft Spinner-bait; (2) Mister Twister Meeny jig; (3) Original Floating Rapala minnow plug; (4) Culprit Wienee Worm; (5) Culprit Jerk Worm, a soft stickbait; (6) Yakima Hawg Boss Super Toad, a deep-diving crankbait; (7) live sucker on a split-shot rig.

Lake Cumberland:

Smallmouth Bass

Lake Cumberland's nearby sister lake, Dale Hollow Reservoir, is arguably the top trophy smallmouth lake in the country. Besides the current world record, just an ounce short of 12 pounds, the lake has produced at least five others over 10. Cumberland is not far behind, with several smallmouths around the 9-pound mark.

Surprisingly, the biggest smallmouths are taken in winter, from mid-November to mid-March. Look for them on rocky main-lake points at the junction of creek arms, usually at depths of 25 to 35 feet. Live 4- to 6-inch creek chubs or suckers, lip-hooked on a split-shot rig, account for most of the big ones. Simply cast the bait out, wait for it to reach bottom, then inch it in ever so slowly.

When the water begins to warm in spring, most smallmouths abandon the points and begin working their way up the creek arms. But they don't go as far up as largemouths or spots, and they stay in deeper water, usually 15 to 25 feet, until spawning time. The most effective pre-spawn technique is casting deep-diving crankbaits over points and along steep banks.

Spawning begins in mid-April. The fish nest over a bottom of broken shale, pea gravel or small rock, usually at depths of 6 to 10 feet, considerably deeper than largemouths or spots. A few fish spawn on main-lake points with a gravel bottom and scattered boulders. Spawning activity continues through mid-May.

Smallmouths are more aggressive than largemouths or spots at spawning time; catch them by twitching a floating minnow plug or soft stickbait (opposite page) over their beds.

How to Work a Soft Stickbait

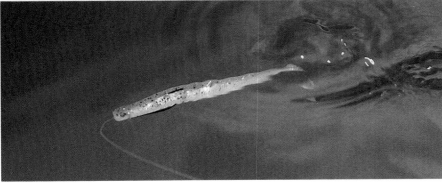

RETRIEVE a soft stickbait with 12- to 18-inch twitches, starting with your rod at 7 o'clock and moving it to 6 o'clock (right). Pause briefly between twitches. This motion gives the worm an enticing side-to-side gliding action (left).

Tips for Finding Smallmouth

CHUNK ROCK holds lots of smallmouths in summer, when they're feeding heavily on crayfish. The broken rock provides ideal crayfish cover.

LIVE TREES, especially willows, growing on rocky points draw summertime smallmouths early and late in the day. In midday, the fish slide into deeper water off the points.

After spawning, smallmouths concentrate on points in the main creek arms. You can catch some fish at depths of 10 to 15 feet during the day, but they usually bite better at night. Cast a ¼-ounce single-blade spinnerbait up to the bank; the fish generally hold at depths of 1 to 5 feet.

By early June, most smallmouths have worked their way to outer creek-arm points or to long main-lake points and reefs that top out at 20 to 30 feet. The fish gradually slide deeper as the water warms, and some of them suspend. By early July, most of them are at depths of 20 to 30 feet; by mid-August, 30 to 60 feet. As a rule, big smallmouths hang much deeper than small ones.

Like spotted bass, smallmouths are easiest to catch at night in summer. Using the same type of spinnerbait as in the post-spawn period, cast over a point or reef and allow the lure to helicopter down 15 to 25 feet before starting your retrieve.

In September, cooling water begins to draw smallmouths shallower, and some of them move back into the creek arms. The smaller fish move in first and the big ones follow a few weeks later.

Using ¼-ounce curlytail jigs or weenie worms on split-shot rigs, work depths of 10 to 15 feet on points and flats adjacent to the creek channel. You can catch fish in these areas through December.

From late fall through the pre-spawn period, smallmouths usually bite best in late afternoon, when the water temperature peaks. Mornings are better from spawning time until early summer, when the fish begin feeding heavily at night. Keep in mind, however, that you can catch some smallmouths at night throughout the year, especially when daytime conditions have been clear and calm.

For live-bait, minnow-plug, weenie-worm or jig fishing, use a 6- to 6½-foot, medium-power spinning outfit and 6- to 8-pound mono. For crankbaiting and spinnerbaiting, a 6- to 6½-foot, medium-power baitcasting outfit with 8- to 10-pound mono is a better choice. The lack of submerged timber in Lake Cumberland makes it possible to get away with light tackle.

Lake Cumberland:
Walleye

Cumberland's cool waters hold an excellent population of walleyes, but they're virtually untouched by anglers. Although some are taken incidentally, usually by striper fishermen, few people actually target the lake's walleyes.

Traditional walleye structure, such as points, humps and irregular breaklines, may hold a few fish, but these places don't offer a permanent food supply. As a result, the fish are nomads, pursuing schools of shad in open water.

This roving behavior accounts for the anglers' lack of interest. Even if they do locate a school, there's little chance the fish will be in the same place the next day.

But the walleyes' taste for shad can also work to your advantage. At night, schools of the baitfish congregate around bright lights, such as those on docks and along the dam face, and walleyes move in for an easy meal. Try casting with a crankbait or weight-forward spinner or a jig tipped with a nightcrawler or shiner. A slip-bobber rig baited with a shiner or shad also works well for night fishing.

Walleye-fishing Tips

CAST a weight-forward spinner tipped with a night-crawler along brushy shorelines and retrieve slowly so the lure bumps the brushtops. The combination of noise, flash and scent will draw fish out of the tangle.

LOOK for walleyes along gently sloping clay banks, especially those with submerged trees or brush. Wave action against the bank keeps clay in suspension, so the clarity remains low enough for the light-sensitive fish.

WORK riprap shorelines near the dam in early morning, late evening or at night. Walleyes are most likely to move into these areas when the wind has been blowing in, particularly after it blows in for 2 or 3 days.

Other Common Gamefish

BLUEGILLS spawn in the back ends of small, shallow creek arms in spring, the best time for good-sized fish. You can catch bluegills the rest of the year in flooded shoreline brush. Effective baits are worms, crickets and grubworms.

WHITE BASS move far up the creek arms in spring. Anglers look for fish breaking the surface and cast to them using small jigging spoons, vibrating plugs and top-waters. Most of the fish weigh a pound or less.

CRAPPIES are easily caught in spring, when they move into shallow creek arms to spawn. Dangle a minnow, either on a small jig or beneath a float, into brush piles. The fish seldom exceed a pound.

TROUT, including rainbows up to 14 pounds and browns up to 18, are caught all year in the tailwaters of the Wolf Creek Dam. Productive lures include minnow plugs, spinners, dry flies and nymphs.

Prairie Reservoirs

Giant reservoirs now sprawl over country where once the largest body of water was a prairie pothole

Besides the huge man-made lakes on the upper Missouri River, this family of reservoirs includes many smaller bodies of water throughout the plains states and prairie provinces.

Most of these lakes are surrounded by gently rolling, fertile prairie. Runoff from these lands carries large amounts of nutrient-rich sediment into the lakes, meaning high fish production.

Known primarily for their outstanding walleye fisheries, prairie reservoirs support a surprising variety of fish life, ranging from channel catfish to chinook salmon to smallmouth bass.

The high sediment load usually results in fertile, low-clarity water at the upper end of the lake. If the basin is long and narrow, as most are, much of the sediment settles out before reaching the lower lake, so the water there is clear and infertile.

As a result of the fertility difference, warmwater gamefish usually grow faster and reach much greater sizes in the upper lake. But coldwater species may thrive in the frigid depths of the lower lake.

Because the climate is fairly dry, tributaries are scarce along the main river, although there are many dry washes. The reservoir has few major creek arms, but an abundance of smaller, shorter creek arms.

During a prolonged drought period, the water level in these lakes may drop 50 feet or more, resulting in problems for fish and fishermen. Spawning areas go dry, and habitat for coldwater gamefish and most species of forage fish shrinks.

When the water drops this low, boat landings are left high and dry, and traditional fishing spots stop producing.

Except for boulders and a little flooded timber, cover in most prairie lakes is limited. There may be some flooded shoreline grasses and brush, however, but only in years of normal or high water.

The expanses of open water in the main-lake basins, combined with the relatively flat terrain and the windy weather typical of the plains states, means rough water much of the time. Most anglers use large, deep-V boats, often equipped with marine radios, for safety.

Case Study:

Lake Sakakawea, North Dakota

Also known as the Garrison Reservoir, Lake Sakakawea is North Dakota's largest body of water. From Williston on the west to Garrison on the east, the lake spans 180 miles of North Dakota prairie.

The Garrison Dam, 2½ miles in length, was completed in 1956, creating the eighth largest reservoir (by volume) in North America (p. 12).

Lake Sakakawea is one of six mainstem U.S. Army Corps of Engineers reservoirs on the Upper Missouri River. Fort Peck Reservoir lies upstream of Lake Sakakawea, in western Montana; Oahe Reservoir, Lake Francis Case and Lake Sharpe lie downstream in South Dakota; and Lewis and Clark Reservoir lies farthest downstream, on the South Dakota-Nebraska border.

These reservoirs were built to control flooding and to supply water for irrigation and hydroelectric power. They also provide water to maintain adequate levels for navigation in the Lower Missouri River and for municipal and industrial purposes.

These reservoirs have greatly benefited fish and waterfowl populations, creating tremendous hunting and fishing opportunities.

Most of the fish species in the lakes today, except for salmon, trout and smallmouth bass, were in the Missouri River originally, but their numbers were considerably less. Waterfowl use the huge lakes as resting areas after feeding in surrounding farm fields.

But flooding of woodlands and brushlands along the river eliminated thousands of acres of prime white-tailed deer, wild turkey, pheasant and sharptail grouse habitat, and flooding of river sandbars has threatened populations of some shorebirds.

Lake Sakakawea is more than a widening of the Upper Missouri River. The Van Hook Arm extends to the North; the Little Missouri Arm, to the west. Lake Audubon (opposite page), though separate from Sakakawea, was also created by the Garrison Dam.

Like the rugged terrain surrounding the reservoir, the lake basin has an abundance of sandy ridges and knolls with patches of gravel and rock. The sandy shorelines erode easily, creating many sheer banks and rock slides.

Sakakawea is renowned for its walleye-sauger fishery, particularly its trophy-caliber walleyes. The light fishing pressure, combined with an abundance of

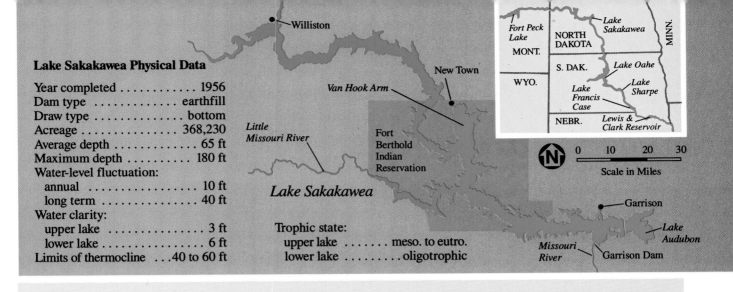

Lake Sakakawea Physical Data

Year completed 1956
Dam type . . . . earthfill
Draw type . . . . bottom
Acreage 368,230
Average depth . . . . 65 ft
Maximum depth . . . . 180 ft
Water-level fluctuation:
    annual . . . . 10 ft
    long term . . . . 40 ft
Water clarity:
    upper lake . . . . 3 ft
    lower lake . . . . 6 ft
Limits of thermocline . . .40 to 60 ft

Trophic state:
    upper lake . . . . meso. to eutro.
    lower lake . . . . oligotrophic

Scale in Miles

Information and Services

General visitor information
North Dakota Parks and Tourism
Capitol Grounds
Bismarck, ND 58505

New Town Chamber of Commerce
Box 422
New Town, ND 58763

Guides
Van Hook Bait and Tackle
(Clayton and Rick Folden)
Box 96
New Town, ND 58763

Kent Odermann
Box 62
Parshall, ND 58770

Accommodations
Indian Hills Resort
Box 700
Garrison, ND 58540

Biologist
North Dakota Game and Fish Department
100 North Bismarck Expressway
Bismarck, ND 58501

Walleyes grow fast on a smelt diet

smelt for food, explains why the fish grow so large. The lake's northern pike also reach tackle-busting size.

Like Fort Peck and Oahe, Sakakawea has enough deep, cold, well-oxygenated water to support salmonids.

Chinook salmon have been stocked by the North Dakota Game and Fish Department since 1982, and more recently, brown and rainbow trout have been introduced. But none of these species can spawn successfully in these waters.

White bass abound in Lake Sakakawea and smallmouth bass have gained a foothold in recent years, but only a few anglers target these species. There's also a small population of crappies, mainly in the creek arms.

The Missouri River system, mainly Sakakawea and Fort Peck, holds one of the country's best paddlefish populations. Few are caught in Sakakawea itself, but snagging is legal in a section of the river upstream of the lake, and fish in the 80- to 100-pound class are taken each year.

Although Sakakawea boasts some of the country's top fishing, it sees comparatively light pressure for its size. Most angling takes place in midsummer, with activity tapering off to practically nothing by late September.

Because of the limited number of anglers and the shortness of the open-water season, the reservoir has only a few full-service resorts. Many anglers stay at small motels near the lake. Guide service, however, is readily available. There are dozens of public boat ramps on Sakakawea, and several on the Fort Berthold Indian Reservation that require a tribal permit. It pays to know where the landings are, especially on windy days. Often you can find one that's sheltered, rather than lose a day of fishing.

Anglers planning a trip to Sakakawea should have a good-sized boat. When the wind whistles across the plains, the lake gets rough in a hurry. Unless you stay within a mile or two of a landing, you'll need at least a 16-foot, deep-V with a 50-hp outboard.

Sakakawea's major problem is low water resulting from prolonged droughts. In the late 80s through the early 90s, the water dropped more than 30 feet, leaving many boat ramps high and dry and seriously affecting gamefish reproduction. A drought is also hard on the smelt crop. The baitfish need cold water to survive, and the volume of cold water diminishes greatly in low-water periods.

Lake Sakakawea Habitat

Main river channel

ROCK SLIDES along steep walls concentrate walleyes and saugers in summer and fall. The saugers run much deeper than the walleyes.

ROCKY MAIN-LAKE POINTS that have extended lips and are near the main river channel hold walleyes and an occasional pike in summer and fall. Saugers hold in deep water off the points.

BACK ENDS of creek arms draw pike in late winter and early spring. The creek arms in the lower lake also hold smallmouths in spring and salmon in fall.

MUD HUMPS near the main river channel draw walleyes in summer and fall. The firm humps remain after the loose sand around them erodes.

SAND ISLANDS, especially those with points dropping into deep water, attract walleyes and saugers in summer and fall.

MAIN CREEK ARMS, especially those in the lower lake, are warmer than the main lake, so they have resident populations of walleyes, pike, smallmouth bass and crappies.

SECONDARY POINTS in the creek arms attract smallmouths most of the year, but they're best during and just after spawning time.

SAND-GRAVEL FLATS that top out at 15 feet or less are good early-summer walleye spots. Saugers hold on deep areas of the flat and off the edges.

RIPRAP along the dam face produces salmon in spring and fall. You'll find smallmouths suspended in deep water off the riprap most of the year.

Lake Sakakawea:
Walleye & Sauger

When the subject of trophy walleyes comes up, Lake Sakakawea is likely to be mentioned early in the conversation. Each year, the lake produces hundreds of 10-pound-plus walleyes.

As a rule, the biggest walleyes are taken in the upper two-thirds of the lake, including the Van Hook Arm. Walleyes do not grow as fast in the deeper, colder water at the lower end.

Saugers receive less attention than walleyes, but they're much more numerous. They run 2 to 3 pounds, with a scattering of 4- to 5-pounders and a few even larger. In fact, Lake Sakakawea produced the current world-record sauger, an 8-pound, 12-ounce giant, in 1971.

The saugeye, a natural walleye-sauger hybrid, also thrives in Sakakawea. Its coloration is intermediate between that of its parents; it has the gold background color of a walleye with the brownish saddle-markings of a sauger. The current world-record saugeye, weighing 12 pounds, 7 ounces, was taken in the Yellowstone River, a tributary of the Missouri River just above Lake Sakakawea.

Most walleyes spawn in large bays in the upper end of the lake, above the confluence of the Little Missouri. In mid-April, just before spawning time, they feed heavily along rocky shorelines in the vicinity of their spawning areas, normally at depths of 2 to 8 feet. Cast to them with ⅛- to ¼-ounce jigs, tipped

Big saugers abound in Sakakawea

with a minnow or soft-plastic curlytail. Toss the jig right into shore and retrieve it with very slow, short hops.

You can catch pre-spawn walleyes the same way in the lower end of the lake, but the colder water delays the spawning cycle in that area for 10 to 20 days. Walleye action slows once spawning begins.

Saugers start to bite immediately after ice-out. Look for them off rocky points near the old river channel. They're normally at depths of 15 to 25 feet in the morning, dropping down to 50 or 60 feet in midday. Try jigging vertically with a ¼- to ½-ounce jig tipped with a minnow.

Biologists are not sure where saugers spawn, and very few saugers are caught around spawning time. Ripe fish have been collected at depths of 6 to 60 feet, usually several weeks after walleye spawning is completed.

Walleye action picks up a couple of weeks after they finish spawning. By then, the fish are moving away from their spawning areas and scattering over large flats that top out at 15 feet or less. At first, the flats produce mostly males running from 1½ to 3 pounds. The females begin to feed in early June on the upper end; mid- to late June on the lower. Many big walleyes are caught during this post-spawn feeding binge. The flats continue to produce for at least a month.

To cover these expansive flats, try trolling crankbaits that run just deep enough to tick bottom, or spinner rigs and slip-sinker rigs baited with night-crawlers, leeches or minnows. Once you find the fish, toss out a marker and work the area more thoroughly with a ⅛- to ¼-ounce jig tipped with the baits just mentioned or a curlytail.

Saugers start to bite again around mid-June. Work depths of 15 to 25 feet, along breaks adjacent to deep water. Use the same post-spawn techniques as you would for walleyes, but if short strikes are a problem, try the techniques shown on page 110.

After walleyes leave the flats, they begin moving to deeper, better-defined structure. You'll find them around sunken and exposed islands, mud humps, rocky points with extended lips, rock slides along shore, or any other structure that breaks sharply into water at least 50 feet deep. A bottom with some rock or gravel will attract more fish than a pure sand or soft-mud bottom.

Most walleyes are caught at depths of 15 to 25 feet in summer, but it's not unusual to find them as deep as 50 feet, especially when the water is clearer than normal. Use the same techniques as you would in the post-spawn period.

Look for summertime saugers on the same structure as walleyes, but in deeper water, usually 30 to 50 feet and occasionally as deep as 70. Jigging vertically with a ¼- to ½-ounce jig tipped with a minnow continues to produce through late fall.

Walleyes move much shallower as the water cools in fall. The year's strongest big-fish pattern develops

LURES for walleyes and saugers include: (1) slip-sinker rig with leech; (2) spinner rig with nightcrawler on bottom-bouncer setup; (3) Northland Whistler Jig and min-now; (4) Northland Fireball Jig and minnow; (5) Mister Twister Meeny jig; (6) Rapala Shad Rap, a medium-running crankbait; (7) Jigging Rapala, for ice fishing.

when walleyes move onto rocky, windswept points near the old river channel or other deep water. Wind blowing into these points draws walleyes into depths of 2 to 5 feet, where you can catch them on ⅛- to ¼-ounce jigs tipped with minnows or curlytails. This pattern holds until freeze-up.

Treacherous ice limits the amount of winter fishing in parts of Sakakawea, but you can catch walleyes and saugers in the same spots as in summer. The action is fastest in the first few weeks after freeze-up. Tip-ups baited with minnows account for most of the fish, but jigging is gaining in popularity.

As in most relatively clear walleye waters, the fish tend to bite best in low-light conditions – early or late in the day, or when skies are overcast. Wind also plays a major role. Waves pounding into a rocky point, shoreline or reef roil the water, creating a mudline (p. 110) that draws in baitfish and soon, walleyes. The longer the wind blows from the same direction, the more likely walleyes will gather and feed heavily on windswept structure. Even after the wind subsides, walleyes often remain for a day or two.

Many Sakakawea walleye-sauger anglers carry three different rod-and-reel combos: a 5½- to 6-foot, medium-power baitcasting outfit with 8- to 12-pound mono, for crankbait and spinner fishing; a 6- to 6½-foot, medium-power, soft-tip spinning outfit with 6-pound mono, for slip-sinker fishing; and a 5½- to 6-foot, medium-power, fast-tip spinning outfit with 6-pound mono, for jig fishing.

Winter walleyes love jigging lures, such as a Swedish Pimple Vingla

How to Jig a Windswept Point

LOOK for a rocky point with an extended lip near the old river channel or other deep water. The fish are most likely to be there if the waves have been pounding in for at least two days.

MAKE a drift past the point to locate the fish. Cast the jig right up to shore and work it back in short hops. Don't use a jig heavier than ¼ ounce; otherwise, you'll snag up too much.

ANCHOR the boat when you find the fish, and work the point thoroughly. If the wind is blowing across the point, the fish will most likely be on the upwind side (dotted line).

Tips for Catching Short-striking Saugers

USE a short-shanked jig, such as a Northland Fireball (top), when tipping with a minnow. The total length is shorter than that of an ordinary jig and minnow (bottom), meaning fewer short strikes. Fireballs and some other jigs come with optional stinger hooks, which clip onto the jig head, to catch short strikers.

PUSH a long-shanked jig hook through the minnow's mouth and out just behind the head. This way, the jig hook is closer to the bait's tail, improving the odds of hooking short strikers.

AVOID tipping with minnows that are too large. If your minnow comes back with the skin ripped on the tail, try tipping your jig with a smaller minnow or a plain soft-plastic curlytail.

Other Walleye-Sauger Tips

KEEP your rod tip low (left) when jigging in a strong wind. If you hold it high (right), the wind will put a large bow in your line, making it hard to feel a strike.

LOOK for wind-induced mudlines, especially around shallow, rocky points. Walleyes feed heavily in the discolored water, even in midday.

Lake Sakakawea:
Smallmouth Bass

Most Sakakawea anglers are so tuned in to walleye fishing, they're unaware of the lake's blossoming smallmouth bass fishery.

Although smallmouths grow slowly in Sakakawea's cool waters, there's plenty of them, particularly in the lower lake. On a good day, you might catch 50. The lake has produced fish over 5 pounds, but anything over 3 is considered large.

When the surface temperature edges into the 60s, usually in early June, smallmouths move into the backs of creek arms to spawn. You can catch them at depths of 3 to 10 feet, and occasionally as deep as 20, using a slip-sinker or slip-bobber rig baited with a 2- to 3-inch minnow or a nightcrawler. Or, cast to them with small lures, such as $1/16$- to $1/4$-ounce horsehead or curlytail jigs, $1/4$-ounce tailspins or vibrating blades, in-line spinners with a size 1 to 3 blade and $1\frac{1}{2}$- to 2-inch crankbaits.

By mid-July, most of the fish have completed spawning and moved farther down the creek arms or into the main lake. Work steep, rough-bottomed structure near water at least 30 feet deep, using the same baits and lures as in spring. You'll catch most fish at depths of 6 to 12 feet, although some may go as deep as 20, especially after a cold front.

Smallmouths begin to form tight schools in deep water when the surface temperature drops below 55°F. They usually hold at depths of 25 to 35 feet in "V"s, shallow creek channels running down the creek arms. Anglers using slip-sinker rigs baited with 2- to 3-inch minnows catch smallmouths until just before freeze-up.

LURES for smallmouths include: (1) Blakemore Road Runner, a horsehead jig; (2) Mann's Little George, a tailspin; (3) slip-bobber rig with minnow; (4) Worden's Rooster Tail, an in-line spinner; (5) Bomber Model "A," a medium-running crankbait; (6) Heddon Sonar, a vibrating blade; (7) slip-sinker rig with nightcrawler.

Dead bait accounts for most Sakakawea pike

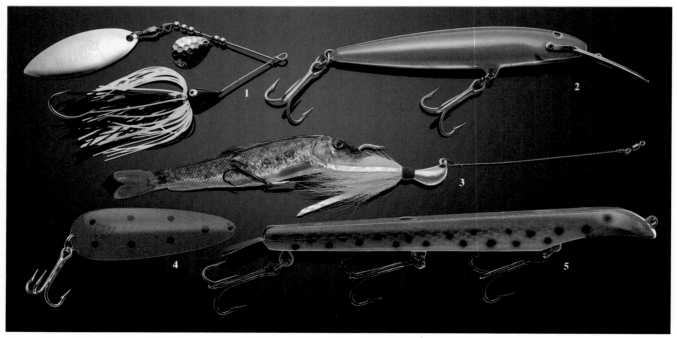

LURES for pike include: (1) Blue Fox Roland Martin Big Bass Spinnerbait; (2) Rapala Magnum, a deep-diving minnow plug; (3) Northland Sting'r Bucktail with sucker; (4) Eppinger Dardevle; (5) Suick Muskie Thriller jerkbait.

Lake Sakakawea:

Northern Pike

Despite the fact that Sakakawea produces dozens of 20-pounders and a few 30s each year, northern pike barely rate a mention among local anglers. But this disinterest means a tremendous opportunity for those who want to catch a real trophy.

The very best time for big pike is the period just before to just after ice-out. The fish feed heavily prior to spawning, and ice-fishermen often enjoy spectacular big-fish action.

Pike begin moving into the creek arms weeks before ice-out. The best arms have an active feeder creek and a well-defined creek channel.

The ice-fishing technique is simple: rig a dead smelt or live sucker on a tip-up and let the bait dangle a few feet beneath the ice. Be sure to spool up with braided Dacron line, at least 30-pound test, in case you hook a big one.

Smelt are available at grocery stores, but many anglers, while ice fishing for pike, catch their own

smelt using a minnow tail on a size 10 hook. Smelt from 7 to 10 inches long work best; they also can be frozen for later use.

You can catch pike in the creek arms for several weeks after ice-out. Using a 6½- to 7-foot, medium-heavy baitcasting outfit with 15- to 20-pound mono, cast out a dead smelt on a slip-sinker rig. Put your rod in a holder so the fish can't pull it in, then sit back and relax.

The bigger pike move out of the creek arms by mid- to late May, when the water approaches 60°F. They scatter into the main lake, where they can find cooler water and an abundance of smelt and goldeyes. Some pike may stay in the creek arms all year, especially when the water is high.

When a June rise floods shoreline grasses in creek arms, anglers catch pike by working the grass beds with spinnerbaits, spoons, jerkbaits and jigs tipped with minnows.

Finding big northerns in summer and fall is tough, but salmon trollers take a few pike when fishing with downriggers in deep water, and walleye fishermen catch an occasional pike on rocky points near the old river channel. Pike specialists sometimes work these points with deep-diving minnow plugs, jerkbaits and jig-minnow combinations.

As a rule, pike are much more active on calm, sunny days than on cold, windy, overcast days. Weather seems to affect their activity more than time of day.

How to Rig and Fish Dead Smelt

HOOK the rear treble in the smelt's head; the sliding treble in the tail. Use a ⅜-ounce slip-sinker rig with a 2-foot, 30-pound, braided-wire leader.

SET your rod in a well-secured rod holder so a fish cannot pull it into the water. Leave the reel in free spool, with the clicker on.

SLIDE an empty shotgun shell over the end of the rod. This way, when a pike swims off with your bait, the shell will pop off, signaling a bite.

Lake Sakakawea:
Salmon

TRY shore fishing if the surface temperature is below 60°F. Shore fishing peaks in fall, as salmon begin looking for a tributary in which to spawn. As spawning time nears, they gradually lose their silvery sheen and turn brownish.

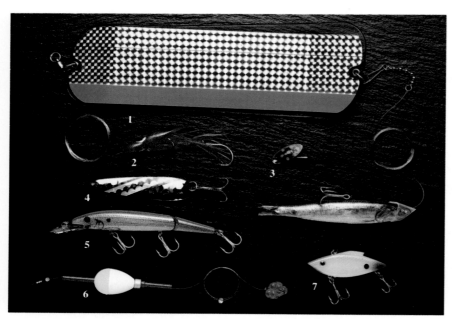

LURES AND BAITS include: (1) O'ki Tackle Big Shooter Flasher with Rhys Davis Anchovy Special hooded-teaser rig; (2) Zak Tackle Wally Whale Squid, also fished with a flasher; (3) Panther Martin spinner; (4) Northern King trolling spoon; (5) Rebel Fastrac floating minnow plug; (6) slip-bobber rig with spawn bag; (7) Bill Lewis Rat-L-Trap, a sinking vibrating plug.

The idea of catching Pacific salmon on the North Dakota prairie may seem strange, but chinooks thrive in Lake Sakakawea, thanks to a major stocking effort by the North Dakota Department of Game and Fish.

Salmon were a natural candidate for filling the void in Sakakawea's cold depths. An efficient deep-water predator was needed to make use of the exploding smelt population.

Although Sakakawea's salmon do not grow quite as large as those in the Great Lakes, they provide a nice change of pace for anglers who would otherwise fish for nothing but walleyes. Most of the fish run 3 to 8 pounds; the current lake record is 24 pounds, 8 ounces.

In early season, the cold water allows salmon to scatter throughout the lake. In years of normal to high run-off, smelt migrate to the upper end of the lake in spring, and the salmon follow. Trollers pulling spoons and crankbaits catch a few salmon, usually at depths of 30 feet or less, on shallow flats near deep water.

When trolling in shallow water, use planer boards to get your lines well to the side of the boat's wake. Otherwise, the boat will spook most of the fish. The collapsible boards shown on the opposite page will easily pull 75 feet to the side. They'll remain stable even in rough water, and when not in use, they fold neatly to conserve space.

In spring, shorefishermen casting spoons and spinners also catch a few salmon, mainly off the riprap along the dam face, and walleye anglers occasionally catch a salmon by accident.

Most salmon hunters don't bother going out until late July, when warming water in the upper lake concentrates salmon at depths of 80 to 130 feet in the lower lake. Anglers trolling flashy or bright-colored spoons, plugs or flasher-squid combinations on downriggers have a good chance of connecting. Another popular trolling rig is a hooded teaser with a dead herring or anchovy. The hood can be adjusted so the bait spins at the desired rate.

For downrigger or trolling-board fishing, use a 7½- to 8-foot, medium-power rod and a level-wind reel that holds at least 250 yards of 14-pound mono. Select a reel with a smooth drag; salmon make long, powerful runs.

A good graph helps you find salmon and avoid snagging submerged timber. Once you mark a few fish or a large plume of smelt, lower your downriggers until the cannonballs are about 10 feet above the salmon or baitfish. This way, your lures will track just above the fish, where they can easily see them.

Many anglers make the mistake of lowering the cannonballs to the level of the fish. The lures then track beneath the fish, where they won't be seen.

A trolling-speed indicator will improve your lure presentation by allowing you to maintain a consistent speed, regardless of wind conditions. Before letting your lure out, pull it alongside the boat to determine the speed that produces the best action.

When the surface temperature drops into the upper 50s, usually in late September, salmon move into creek arms adjacent to the old river channel in an attempt to find a spawning stream. There are no streams large enough for spawning, but this movement pattern gives shorefishermen a good chance to catch salmon.

When the fish first move in, they'll hit artificials, including spoons, minnow plugs, vibrating plugs and crankbaits. But as spawning time approaches, you'll do better on spawn bags fished 1 to 5 feet beneath a bobber.

Chinooks almost always bite best in early morning, from one-half hour before to two hours after sunrise, or maybe a little longer on cloudy days. After that, the salmon go deeper and feeding slows. They turn on again toward evening. An approaching front also seems to activate the fish.

How to Make a Collapsible Planer Board

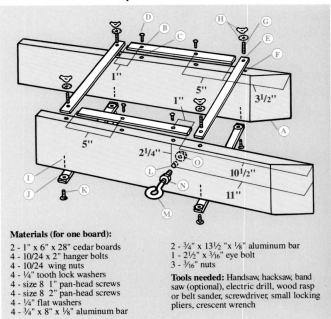

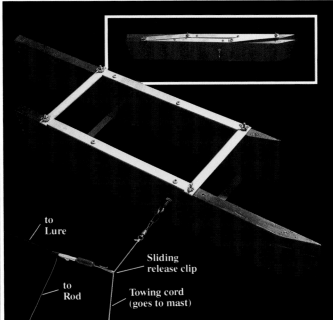

Materials (for one board):
2 - 1" x 6" x 28" cedar boards
4 - 10/24 x 2" hanger bolts
4 - 10/24 wing nuts
4 - ¼" tooth lock washers
4 - size 8 1" pan-head screws
4 - size 8 2" pan-head screws
4 - ¼" flat washers
4 - ¾" x 8" x ⅛" aluminum bar

2 - ¾" x 13½ "x ⅛" aluminum bar
1 - 2½" x ³⁄₁₆" eye bolt
3 - ³⁄₁₆" nuts

Tools needed: Handsaw, hacksaw, band saw (optional), electric drill, wood rasp or belt sander, screwdriver, small locking pliers, crescent wrench

CUT one end of each board at (A) a 30-degree angle, using band saw or handsaw. Smooth taper with wood rasp or belt sander. Using measurements shown, drill (B) two ³⁄₁₆-inch holes in each long aluminum bar. Place bars on top edges of the boards, and drill (C) ⅛-inch pilot holes through holes in bar and into wood; attach each bar with (D) 1-inch screws. Drill (E) two ³⁄₁₆-inch holes ⅜ inch from ends of each short bar; lay two bars across tops of boards so they butt against ends of long bars, and drill (F) ⅛-inch pilot holes through holes in short bars and into wood. Using a locking pliers, screw (G) hanger bolts into pilot holes; place short bars over bolts, and add (H) lock

washers and wing nuts. Lay short bars across bottom of boards, directly below top bars, and drill (I) ⅛-inch pilot holes through holes in bars and into wood. Place (J) a flat washer under holes in each bottom bar, then attach bars with (K) 2-inch screws. Drill (L) a ³⁄₁₆-inch hole for (M) eye bolt at position shown, screw (N) nut onto eye bolt, insert eye bolt through hole, then add (O) two more nuts and tighten with wrench. To use trolling board, attach towing cord (p. 116) to eye bolt, and let out the board. Then let out your line, attach it to sliding release clip, and allow clip to slide down cord as shown. To fold up board (inset), loosen wing nuts and lift short bars enough to clear long bars.

Rigging Small Boats for Salmon Fishing

Many Sakakawea anglers, particularly walleye fishermen, use tiller-operated boats from 16 to 18 feet long. But trying to fish with downriggers from this type of boat can be a problem. Normally, anglers mount their downriggers on a board across the transom, and when a fish strikes, everyone rushes to the back of the boat to crank up the cannonballs and land the fish. Not only is crowding a problem, the extra weight in the rear could allow waves to wash over the transom.

The rigging method shown here solves these problems. By mounting long-arm downriggers farther forward, as shown, passengers can comfortably operate the downrigger on their side of the boat. The driver has plenty of room to run the boat, and the boat is well balanced so water won't pour in. As long as the driver keeps the boat on a fairly straight course as the lines are being set, there is no chance of getting them in the motor. Once the lines are set, they're deep enough so the boat can make sharp turns.

Following are descriptions of the equipment needed for this rigging method:

MAST. A pole elevating the cord that pulls the planer boards. This model comes with reels that make it easy to let out cord. After the board is out, back up the crank to lock the reel. Then let out your line and attach the sliding clip as shown on p. 115.

LONG-ARM DOWNRIGGERS. The downriggers shown here are computerized electric models, but any long-armed downriggers will do. Look for models with built-in rod holders.

SWIVEL-TYPE ROD HOLDERS. You may need extra rod holders when fishing with downriggers and planer boards (above). Swivel-type holders are handy because they can be adjusted to any angle and lock firmly in place.

ROD-STORAGE RACKS. To prevent breakage when moving from spot to spot, store the rods in vertical storage racks.

ANTENNA. You'll need an antenna for both your Loran and marine radio. With this combination model, however, you need only a single antenna.

ELECTRONICS. A (1) good graph helps you locate salmon and baitfish and track the cannonballs. This video also gives surface temperature and trolling speed information. A (2) Loran-C unit helps you navigate in the fog and return to good spots. A (3) marine radio is recommended for safety and comes in handy for exchanging fishing information.

CHANNEL CATFISH can be caught in the backs of creek arms that have feeder creeks, either active or intermittent. The fish run 1½ to 3 pounds, but 10- to 15-pounders are not uncommon.

WHITE BASS are most numerous in the upper two-thirds of the lake. They run from 1 to 1½ pounds.

RAINBOW TROUT are usually caught incidentally by anglers fishing for salmon or walleyes in the lower lake. They average about 2 pounds, with an occasional fish up to 5.

BROWN TROUT are also caught occasionally by salmon or walleye anglers, usually in the lower half of the lake.

Canyon Reservoirs

Some of the biggest trout taken anywhere in the world come from these deep, gin-clear waters

I mpounded with spectacular dams measuring up to 700 feet high, canyon reservoirs are the deepest, coldest, clearest type of man-made lake. Usually formed in narrow valleys between high mountains, these waters offer some of the most breathtaking scenery on earth.

Most canyon reservoirs were built for the main purpose of generating hydro-electric power. Their great depth means they have a tremendous *head*. Because the water must drop so far, it produces more energy than it would were the dam lower. Canyon reservoirs also have a massive storage capacity for irrigation and municipal water supply.

Those reservoirs used primarily for power generation have fairly stable water levels, fluctuating no more than 20 feet during an average year. But canyon reservoirs used for flood control may fluctuate nearly 100 feet from the draw-down mark in late fall to the high-water mark in spring.

The main body of a canyon reservoir is long and narrow, as are the creek arms. Often, the two are difficult to distinguish. Steep rock walls are the primary fish cover, although there may be a little flooded timber on points and in the back ends of creek arms.

Found mainly in the western United States, canyon reservoirs are fed primarily by snowmelt from the mountains. Most of these lakes have very low fertility levels and are classed as oligotrophic. But the upper ends may be highly fertile, if inflowing streams carry heavy nutrient loads from nearby farmlands or cities. In some of these lakes, the upper ends have dense algal blooms and the depths lose their oxygen in summer.

The low fertility, combined with cold water and sharp-sloping shorelines, makes most canyon reservoirs inhospitable to warmwater fish species. Even if the fish can find good spawning areas, they grow slowly because of the limited food supply.

The fact that many of these lakes are at high altitudes adds to the problem of slow growth. Air temperatures are colder than normal and the growing season is relatively short.

But coldwater species, such as rainbow, brown, cutthroat and lake trout, thrive in many canyon reservoirs. Because the depths are well oxygenated, the fish can descend to whatever level has a comfortable temperature. Salmon, particularly kokanee, have been stocked in some of these lakes, but they grow slowly compared to sea-run salmon.

119

Case Study:

Flaming Gorge Reservoir, Utah & Wyoming

When the sun hits the reddish walls at the entrance to Flaming Gorge Canyon, you'll immediately know how the lake got its name.

Completed in 1964, Flaming Gorge Dam was constructed by the Bureau of Reclamation as part of the Colorado River Storage Project. The spectacular concrete arch dam, which is more than 500 feet high, impounded Utah's Green River for the main purposes of generating power and storing water to maintain adequate flow downstream.

The reservoir consists of three areas, each with different characteristics.

The upper, or inflow, area is the warmest, shallowest and most fertile part of the reservoir. About 39 miles long, it supports good numbers of channel catfish and smallmouth bass, with an abundance of forage fish, mainly suckers and Utah chubs. During cold-water periods, trout and salmon move into the lower reaches of this zone to feed on the plentiful forage.

Entrance to Flaming Gorge Canyon

Flaming Gorge is capable of producing lake trout like this – and bigger

The lower zone, or canyon area, extends 24 miles to the dam at Dutch John, Utah. With steep, rock walls and clear, cold, infertile water more than 400 feet deep, this area is best suited to rainbow trout and kokanee salmon.

The middle zone, about 28 miles long, is a transition area, with intermediate characteristics.

Known as the Open Hills area, the middle zone has gently sloping shorelines, numerous bays and water as deep as 200 feet. This habitat is best for lake trout, kokanees and smallmouths.

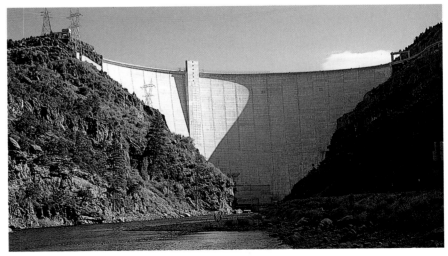

Flaming Gorge Dam

The inflow area

The Open Hills area

Famed for its huge brown trout in years past, Flaming Gorge produced a world-record brown weighing 33 pounds, 10 ounces in 1977. But browns have virtually disappeared from the lake, mainly because of food competition from Utah chubs (p. 136).

Today, Flaming Gorge Reservoir is considered one of the top trophy lake trout fisheries in the United States. The fish commonly grow to 30 pounds or more on a diet consisting primarily of Utah chubs and kokanee salmon.

In 1979, a multi-level draw was installed in the Flaming Gorge Dam, making it possible to discharge water of about 50°F year-round and to stock stream trout in the tailwaters area. The Green River, from the dam downstream to the Colorado border, is now considered a world-class trout fishery, with an abundance of good-sized rainbow, brown and cutthroat trout, as well as some rainbow-cutthroat hybrids and a few brook trout.

Besides fishing, other popular activities on the lake include pleasure boating and waterskiing. Although there are no resorts or lodges, the lake has numerous campgrounds, 3 privately owned marinas and many public boat ramps.

The canyon area

Flaming Gorge Reservoir Physical Data

Year completed	1964
Dam type	arch
Draw type	multi-level
Acreage	40,020
Average depth	111 ft
Maximum depth:	
upper lake	80 ft
lower lake	440 ft
Water-level fluctuation:	
annual	8 ft
long term	20 ft
Water clarity:	
upper lake	3 ft
lower lake	18 ft
Limits of thermocline	35 to 45 ft
Trophic state:	
inflow	eutrophic
Open Hills	mesotrophic
canyon	oligotrophic

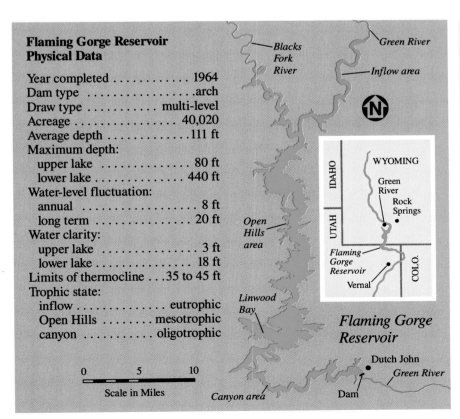

Flaming Gorge Reservoir

Information and Services

General visitor information
Dinosaurland Travel Board
235 East Main
Vernal, UT 84078

Guides
Flaming Gorge Lodge (Herald Egbert)
Greendale
155 US Highway 191
Dutch John, UT 84023-9702

"Happy Daze" Guide Service (Tony Kaumo)
2736 Commercial Way
Rock Springs, WY 82901

"The Good Life" Guide Service (Cliff Redmon)
Box 173
Lyman, WY 82937

Accommodations
Lucerne Valley Marina
P. O. Box 356
Manila, UT 84046

Biologists
Wyoming Fish & Game Department
351 Astle Ave.
Green River, WY 82935

Utah Dept. of Natural Resources
Flaming Gorge Project
600 South Blvd., P. O. Box 158
Dutch John, UT 84023

Flaming Gorge Habitat

FEEDER CREEKS draw spawning runs of kokanees in fall. Good-sized flats at the mouths of feeder creeks hold plenty of rainbows and some smallmouth bass during the summer.

ROCK RIDGES visible on shore often extend far into the lake and make excellent summertime fish habitat. The shallow portion of a ridge usually holds smallmouth bass; the deeper portion, lake trout.

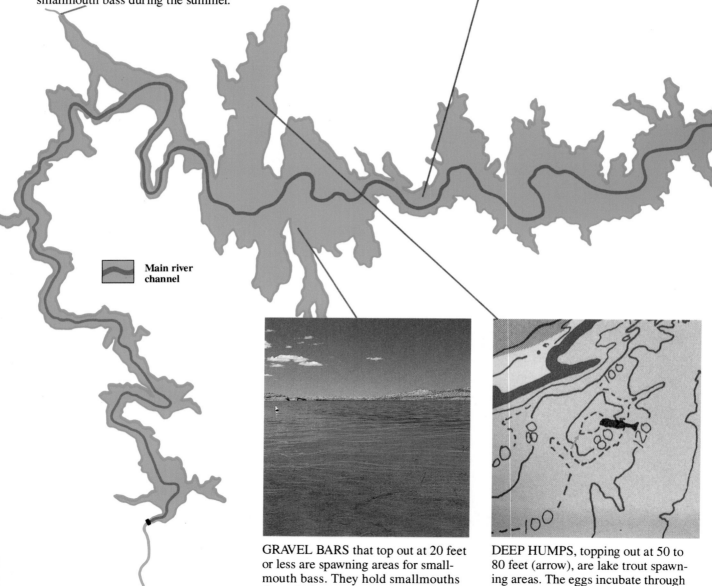

Main river channel

GRAVEL BARS that top out at 20 feet or less are spawning areas for smallmouth bass. They hold smallmouths through the summer and draw rainbow trout in winter.

DEEP HUMPS, topping out at 50 to 80 feet (arrow), are lake trout spawning areas. The eggs incubate through the winter in crevices between the small rocks and hatch in early spring.

SMALL COVES with large crops of Utah chubs and other baitfish draw smallmouth bass in summer. Rainbows often move into the coves on summer mornings and evenings to feed on emerging insects.

GRAVEL SHORELINES, particularly those with a gradual taper, hold smallmouth bass in spring and summer. Those with a sharper slope are good for summertime rainbows, especially in morning and evening.

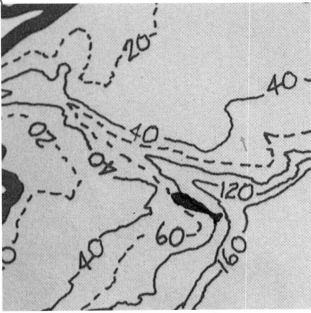

FLATS that top out at 40 to 80 feet (arrow), with deeper water nearby, are top choices for lake trout in summer. Kokanees roam the flats in morning and evening, and the lake trout follow. The trout go deeper in midday.

CLIFF WALLS make ideal feeding areas for kokanees in summer because plankton stacks up along them when the wind blows in. Walls with steplike ledges draw spawning kokanees in fall and rainbows in winter.

Flaming Gorge Reservoir:
Lake Trout

Biologists predict that Flaming Gorge will produce a world-record lake trout in the near future. The reservoir has already yielded three fish over 50 pounds, including a 51-pound, 8-ouncer, caught in 1988.

The fish grow at an incredible rate, thanks to an abundance of forage including kokanee salmon and Utah chubs. A wide slot limit has been established to protect the spawners and to ensure that many of the fish reach a large size before they're harvested. Any lake trout from 26 to 36 inches long (about 8 to 22 pounds) must be released immediately.

Lake trout, called *mackinaws* by local anglers, are easiest to find and catch in October, when they con-

gregate near their spawning areas. Look for gravel humps that top out at 50 to 80 feet adjacent to water at least 100 feet deep. The best spawning humps are in the Open Hills section of the lake. In Linwood Bay, for instance, lake trout spawn on gravel piles left behind when fill was removed during construction of the dam.

Locate fish on spawning humps with a graph or flasher, then vertically jig for them with 1- to 1½-ounce bucktail jigs, airplane jigs or jigging spoons. For best success, tip your jigs with strips of sucker meat. Live baitfish are illegal. A medium-heavy, fast-action baitcasting outfit spooled with 10- to 14-pound mono is ideal for this type of fishing.

After spawning, usually in early November, many lake trout migrate upstream, where forage is more abundant. You'll find them as far north as the junction with the Blacks Fork River.

Ice fishing on Flaming Gorge accounts for nearly one-third of the annual lake trout harvest. Try fishing the

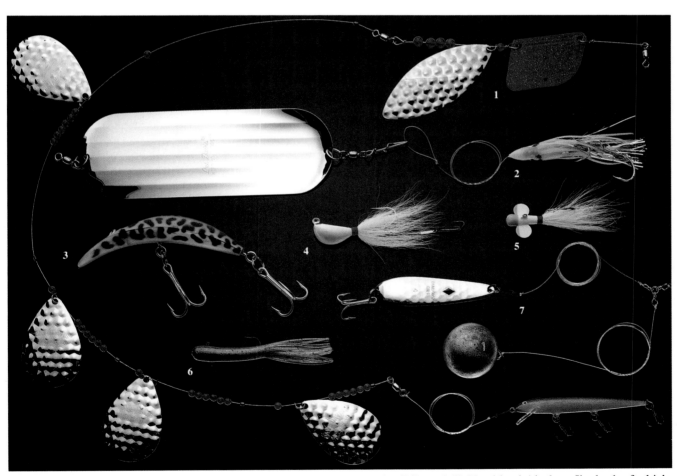

LURES for lake trout include: (1) Les Davis Standard Cowbell rig with Original Floating Rapala minnow plug; (2) Les Davis Herring Dodger with Alpena Trolling Squid; (3) Worden's FlatFish, a trolling plug; (4) Northland Sting'r bucktail jig and (5) Northland Airplane Jig, both of which can be tipped with sucker strips; (6) Stick-O-Pig tube jig; (7) three-way-swivel rig with one-pound lead ball and Luhr-Jensen Diamond King trolling spoon.

humps, shoreline shelves, flats and breaks adjacent to the structure at depths of 40 to 100 feet.

A graph or flasher comes in handy for finding fish in a hurry. Use a stiff, 4-foot rod and a baitcasting reel with 12- to 20-pound mono for jigging with 1- to 1½-ounce bucktail and airplane jigs. Tip them with dead bullheads or chubs, or sucker meat.

When the water begins to warm in April, lake trout return to the Open Hills area and move very little until the next fall. You'll find them on flats adjacent to creek channels or the main river channel, usually at depths of 40 to 80 feet and always near a sharp break. Other prime locations are ridges topping out at 60 to 80 feet with much deeper water on either side.

Jigging also works well in spring and summer, if you can find a concentration of fish with your graph, and if there isn't too much wind. Windy weather makes it difficult to stay on top of the fish and control the depth of your jig.

When fish are scattered along the breaks, trolling with downriggers or wire line works better than vertical jigging.

Downriggers enable you to fish with light tackle and to precisely control the depth of your baits. Soft-tipped, 7½-foot downrigger rods and level-wind reels spooled with 12- to 20-pound mono are ideal. Faster-than-normal trolling speeds (2.6 to 3.2 mph) seem to trigger the lake trout, so most anglers use

Downrigger Trolling for Lake Trout

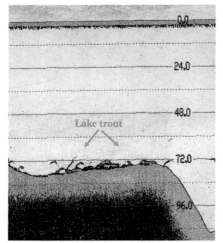

1. LOCATE lake trout with your graph before you start trolling. Usually, they'll be on a flat, near a sharp drop-off.

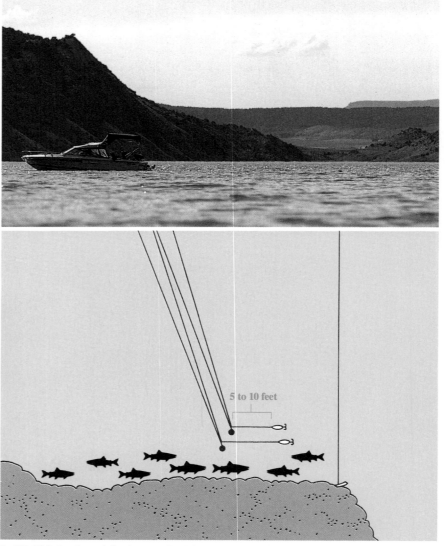

2. TOSS out a marker when you graph some lake trout, but make sure it's off to the side of the fish, not right on top of them.

3. TROLL back and forth over the lake trout school, using the marker as a reference point. Keep your "leads" no longer than 5 or 10 feet so the lures move up and down with the cannonballs. The balls should track just above the fish, not right through the school.

cannonballs weighing at least 10 pounds. This way, the balls don't swing back far enough to have much effect on your depth.

Downrigger trollers rely heavily on natural bait, such as strips of sucker meat fished on salmon squids, and threaded-on suckers and chubs (below). The best artificials are thin trolling spoons and 4-inch floating minnow plugs. These baits and lures are usually fished behind cowbells, or *pop gear*, a series of large spinner blades that serve as an attractor, or behind dodgers.

Wire-line rigs are a good choice for slow-trolling with thin spoons or trolling plugs. Use a heavy 5- to 5½-foot trolling rod with a roller on the tip and a large-capacity, level-wind reel filled with 30- to 40-pound

single-strand wire. Haywire-twist (p.150) the wire onto a three-way swivel. Attach a 1-pound lead ball to the swivel with 2 feet of 20-pound mono; the lure, with 4 feet.

Another option, for those who don't like dragging a heavy weight, is long-lining with 80- to 90-pound wire. By letting out about 200 feet of line, you can get down to the fish, but you'll find it more difficult to follow contours and keep your lure near the bottom.

By far the best time to catch lake trout is from sunrise until about 9 A.M. There's a lesser bite just before sunset. They feed very little when the sun is high. Most anglers prefer overcast skies, but if the clouds are accompanied by strong winds, boat control becomes a serious problem.

Tips for Catching Lake Trout

BOUNCE your cannonballs off the bottom from time to time, especially when the trout are inactive. The puff of silt and the sound may trigger a strike.

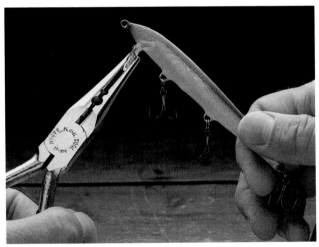

BREAK the lip off a floating minnow plug when trolling it behind a dodger. This prevents the lure from spinning; the dodger provides the action.

TIP a squid with a 3-inch strip of sucker meat when trolling the lure behind a dodger. The combination of larger size, extra action and scent draws more strikes than a plain squid.

THREAD an 18-inch, 20-pound leader with a size 2 treble through a baitfish by attaching the leader to a wire, inserting it behind the vent, and pushing it out the mouth (left). Pull the leader to snug up the hook (right).

129

Flaming Gorge Reservoir:
Kokanee Salmon

Flaming Gorge abounds with kokanee salmon, or "kokes," as local anglers call them. These small salmonids are a landlocked form of red, or sockeye, salmon. Besides providing an excellent sportfishery, they make up a high percentage of the lake trout's food supply.

Most kokes run from 1 to 1½ pounds, but there's a shot at a 3- to 4-pounder. The lake record, a 5-pound, 5-ouncer, was caught in 1984.

Kokes are found mainly in the Open Hills and canyon sections of the lake. Look for them along main-lake cliff walls where the wind piles up plankton, their major food.

The action begins in mid-May, when the surface water reaches the low 50s. Then, you'll find most of the fish at depths of 20 feet or less. But as the water warms, they gradually move deeper. By July, they're often at depths of 40 to 60 feet; by August, as deep as 80 feet.

Anglers trolling small spoons with downriggers or lead-core line (opposite page) account for most of

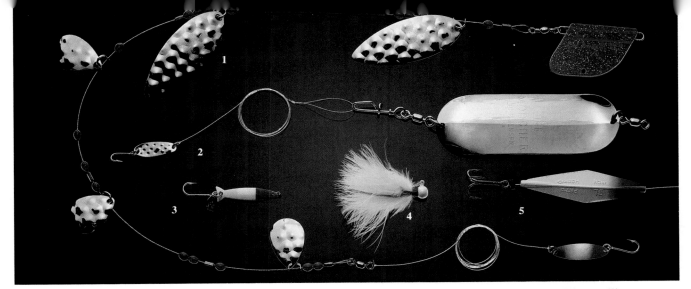

LURES for kokanee salmon include: (1) Dave Davis Cowbell rig with Luhr-Jensen Needlefish trolling spoon; (2), Luhr-Jensen Moocher Dodger and Knobby Wobbler trolling spoon; (3) Luhr-Jensen Kokanee King trolling spoon; (4) Bass Buster Doll Fly, a marabou jig; and (5) Buzz-Bomb, a jigging spoon.

Tips for Catching Kokanees

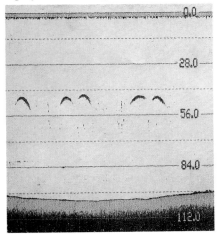

LOOK for kokanees in a precise depth range. The fish on this graph tape are suspended at 45 to 50 feet; troll just above them.

USE metered lead-core line when trolling for kokanees. Experiment to determine which colors equate to different trolling depths.

VERTICALLY JIG on shelves along the cliff walls to catch kokanees around spawning time. Work the lure with short hops.

the fish. You can troll the spoon by itself or behind a dodger or pop gear (p. 129) as an attractor. Use your graph to determine the right trolling depth, and keep your boat about 50 to 100 yards away from the cliff wall. Any kind of light spinning or baitcasting outfit with 6- to 10-pound mono will work for downrigging. For lead-lining, use a 5½-foot, medium-power baitcasting outfit and a reel large enough to hold 100 yards of 13- to 18-pound lead-core.

In early September, kokanees begin moving shallower, edging toward 30-foot shelves on the cliff walls, where they will spawn in October. As spawning time approaches, males develop a distinct hook, or *kype*, on the snout. The body of both sexes turns bright reddish; the head, greenish. Even at depths of 30 feet, you can often see the reddish forms on the

spawning shelves. Kokes also spawn in feeder creeks throughout the reservoir, some of which are closed to fishing at spawning time.

Although the fish don't feed during the spawning period, males are highly aggressive at this time, striking at each other or anything else that gets in their way, including lures.

When you see some fish on a spawning shelf, try vertically jigging with a ¼-ounce jig or jigging spoon. Use medium-power, fast-action spinning gear with 6- to 8-pound mono for this type of fishing.

Kokes bite best in early morning. They're in shallower water then, and they school much more tightly than in midday. On midsummer mornings, you may find fish at depths of 10 to 20 feet.

Pop gear boosts your odds when trolling for rainbows

Flaming Gorge Reservoir:

Rainbow, Brown & Cutthroat Trout

When you see a big rainbow catapult from the water along a canyon wall, you'll know why trout fishing in Flaming Gorge Reservoir, and the Green River below it, is so popular.

The reservoir is well stocked with rainbows and produces an occasional trophy brown trout, a reminder of the 1970s glory years, when the lake produced two world-record browns.

Brown trout dominate in the river, but there's also a good supply of rainbows, cutthroats and *turbos* (p. 135). The trout fishery in the reservoir differs considerably from that in the river. Following are specifics on each type of fishing:

Fishing the Reservoir

Rainbows are the bread-and-butter fish of Flaming Gorge because they're so easy to catch, even by anglers without downriggers or other specialized trolling gear.

Although the average size of the rainbows is less than a pound, the lake has produced fish over 20 pounds. The lake record, caught in 1979, weighed 26 pounds, 2 ounces.

Two different strains of rainbows are stocked in Flaming Gorge. The Eagle Lake strain (from Eagle Lake, California) is a shoreline-oriented fish that rarely goes deeper than 20 feet, making it popular among shorefishermen. The Kamloops strain (from Kamloops Lake, British Columbia) is deeper-bodied and inhabits deeper water.

Trout-fishing Tips

LOOK for dimples on the surface, a sign that rainbows are feeding on insects. You're most likely to see dimples in the morning and evening, when hatches are heaviest.

TROLL with a side planer, especially when trout are in shallow water. A planer carries your lure away from the boat's wake so you can reach fish that haven't been spooked by the motor.

Although the canyon area yields the most rainbows, the Open Hills area sees the earliest action. Rainbows show up in late April, about two weeks earlier than in the canyon. The lower end of the inflow area produces a few rainbows in fall and winter.

There's nothing complicated about rainbow fishing. Using a light spinning outfit with 4- to 6-pound mono, troll with a 2- to 3-inch floating minnow plug, a small spoon, or a small spinner tipped with a piece of nightcrawler. Fish these lures unweighted, with or without pop gear.

For bigger rainbows, you'll have to troll a little deeper, from 15 to 35 feet. Use downriggers and medium-power spinning gear with 6- to 10-pound mono, or a medium-power baitcasting outfit and a large-capacity reel spooled with 13- to 18-pound lead-core line.

A good graph comes in handy for locating rainbows in open water, but you can usually find them by trolling randomly. When you locate a school, try to find a landmark so you can stay with them.

Shorefishermen using light spinning gear with 4- to 6-pound mono catch plenty of rainbows with a worm

LURES for reservoir trout include: (1) Original Floating Rapala; (2) Mepps Aglia spinner; (3) Wazp ice fly and waxworm; (4) size 12 Adams dry fly; (5) casting bubble and crawler; (6) cowbells with Luhr-Jensen Needlefish spoon.

or nightcrawler on a size 6 or 8 Aberdeen hook fished behind a casting bubble. This technique works best on calm mornings and evenings, when the trout are rising in small coves.

Dry-fly fishing is also effective when the trout are rising. Use a 4- to 6-weight fly rod with a floating, weight-forward line, or cast the flies with a light spinning outfit and a casting-bubble rig.

A good share of the rainbows work their way upstream in fall. By early November, you'll find large concentrations along the cliff walls in the upper portion of the Open Hills area. You can catch rainbows by trolling or shorefishing using the techniques mentioned above. They continue to bite until freeze-up.

Rainbows can be caught throughout the day, although they feed most heavily on the surface in morning and evening. The fish also stay closer to the surface on cloudy days.

Anglers also catch good numbers of rainbows through the ice. Try fishing 10- to 15-foot shelves along the bluffs, using a light graphite jigging rod, 4- to 6-pound mono and small ice flies tipped with grubworms.

Mackenzie boats work well for drifting the river

Fishing the Green River

In a recent survey, fisheries workers counted as many as 14,000 trout per mile in the Green River, reconfirming its reputation as one of the country's premier trout streams.

With a population this high, you'd expect the trout to run small, but such is not the case. They average almost 18 inches, and there are a fair number over 10 pounds. The river has yielded rainbows up to 22 pounds and browns up to 20, and local anglers tell of hooking much bigger ones.

To preserve this unique fishery, the Utah Division of Wildlife Resources has established stringent regulations. Live bait of all types is prohibited, and there is a slot limit of 13 to 20 inches, meaning that all trout within that range must be released. You can keep only one trout over 20 inches and two under 13.

Although the tailwater temperature averages about 50°F year around, the trout bite best from April through June, when the mayflies are hatching. Another peak time is September and October, when big browns begin feeding heavily.

Fly fishermen use dry flies, particularly mayfly and caddis fly imitations, nymphs, or terrestrials, such as beetle, grasshopper and ant imitations. The "double-ugly," a local pattern, also works well (opposite page).

One of the most effective methods is drifting the river with a Mackenzie boat or rubber raft, preferably with a guide who can control the boat and help you spot fish.

Using an 8½- to 9-foot, 4- or 5-weight fly rod, a weight-forward floating line, and a 9-foot leader with a 4X to 6X tippet, cast ahead of the boat and toward shore. This way, your fly drifts naturally, without drag, so it doesn't spook the fish.

You can also drift a fly using a light spinning outfit with 4- to 6-pound mono and a casting-bubble rig (p. 133). Or, cast with small spinners, crankbaits or jigs.

Other productive techniques include shorefishing or wading. Most anglers work the east bank, with its 15-mile-long trail, but you'll do better by boating across to the west bank, where fishing pressure is lighter. Drift a fly through fast runs, and if you see trout rising for insects along the bank, try floating a dry fly over them. You can also work pools with spinning lures.

TURBOS, also called cutbows, are rainbow-cutthroat hybrids. They get their name because of the supercharged fight they wage. The river also holds true cutthroats.

BROWN TROUT are the most common gamefish in the Green River. They're much warier and more difficult to catch than the other trout species. Bigger browns, which feed primarily on baitfish, are usually caught around dawn or dusk, or at night.

LURES for tailwater trout include: (1) scud; (2) Elk Hair Caddis; (3) Royal Coachman; (4) Pale Morning Dun, a mayfly imitation; (5) foam beetle and (6) Dave's Hopper, both terrestrial patterns; (7) Super Vibrax spinner; (8) Muddler jig; (9) Original Floating Rapala minnow plug.

How to Tie a "Double-Ugly"

TIE two grizzly (black-and-white striped) hackle feathers onto a size 6 dry-fly hook, just before the bend. Using a hackle pliers (right), wrap them around hook, one hackle at a time.

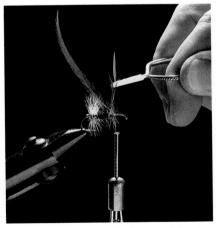

ATTACH three strands of peacock herl (green); wrap forward about 1/4 inch. Tie on two brown hackles; wrap around the center of the hook (shown). Add one more section of peacock and one of grizzly.

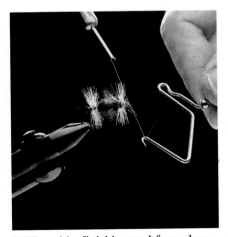

USE a whip-finishing tool for a clean, no-slip knot at the eye of the hook. Trim away any feathers that cover the eye, and dab head cement on the knot for additional strength.

Flaming Gorge Reservoir:

Smallmouth Bass

LURES for smallmouths include: (1) Bill Lewis Rat-L-Top, a propbait; (2) Stanley Jig with pork trailer; (3) Kalin's curlytail grub with ball-head jig; (4) Bagley Top Gun, a shallow-running minnow plug; (5) Rapala Fat Rap, a shallow-running crankbait; (6) Bomber Model "A," a deep-diving crankbait; (7) Super Vibrax spinner.

Originally stocked in 1967 to control the booming population of Utah chubs, smallmouth bass have gained a solid foothold in Flaming Gorge. And they've helped reduce the chub population, which was competing with young trout and salmon for plankton.

But at such a high altitude (6040 feet), the smallmouth growing season is short, meaning that the

BROKEN ROCK POINTS, especially those with a long, shallow lip, are prime summertime smallmouth spots, because they hold large numbers of crayfish and baitfish.

ROCKY REEFS with deep water nearby also hold smallmouths in summer, but are most productive in fall. The fish can feed in the shallow rocks, then slide into deep water to rest.

USE crayfish from 2½ to 3 inches long to catch good-sized smallmouths. Smaller bass will usually avoid crayfish this large. You can easily collect your own crayfish after dark, with the help of a powerful flashlight (left).

One of the best places to find them is on a concrete launching ramp. Rig a crayfish with only a split shot and a size 2 hook inserted through the bottom of the tail and out the top (right).

fish run small. They average less than a pound, with an occasional fish up to 3. The lake record is 4 pounds, 6 ounces.

Smallmouths abound in the upper and middle sections of the reservoir, but are scarce in the canyon area. The vertical rock walls do not provide the "lip" area that the fish need.

In mid-May, anglers begin catching a few smallmouths on rocky points and humps in the upper lake, but the action, particularly for better-sized fish, peaks in June. Then, spawners concentrate on gravel points and bars, shale shelves, and sandy areas in the back ends of creek arms. Using a light spinning outfit with 4- to 6-pound mono, cast to them with spinners, shallow- to medium-running crankbaits or topwaters, especially propbaits. You'll find most of the fish at depths of 2 to 10 feet.

After spawning, smallmouths in the upper lake are found on soft-bottomed flats with sparse weeds.

They're normally at depths of 4 to 8 feet, so you can cast to them with floating minnow plugs, spinners and topwaters.

Smallmouths hold on rocky points and humps the rest of the year, gradually sliding deeper during the summer and fall. But they seldom go deeper than 20 feet. Deep-diving crankbaits and curlytail jigs account for most of the fish in summer and early fall.

Your best chance for big smallmouths is from mid-September to mid-October. Try using larger-than-normal lures and baits, such as a jig-and-pig, or live crayfish (above). The action slows in late October, when the water temperature drops below 50°F.

The Blacks Fork River and the Green River above the reservoir also have excellent, though lightly fished, smallmouth populations. You'll find most of the fish at the heads of deep pools and in eddies behind boulders. Cast to them with spinners and small minnow plugs.

Canadian Shield Reservoirs

These enormous reservoirs top the list of North America's largest man-made lakes

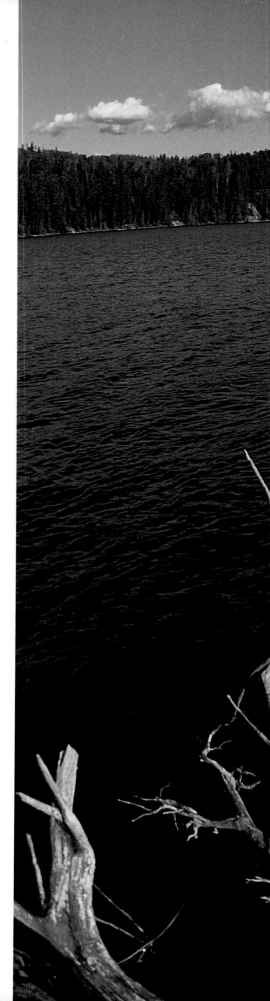

With the multitude of natural lakes on the Canadian Shield, one might ask why it's necessary to create more lakes. The answer: to generate inexpensive hydroelectric power.

Snowmelt and rainfall fill the reservoirs in spring, and the water is gradually drawn off the rest of the year to drive the turbines. The water level usually reaches its lowest point in late winter.

What is now a Canadian Shield reservoir was most likely a large river system with many connecting lakes before construction of the dam. After impoundment, the rising water joined lakes that were part of the river system, as well as separate lakes, to form a much larger body of water.

Reservoirs of this type are found throughout the Canadian Shield, a massive area of exposed bedrock covering much of the eastern half of Canada and extending into the north-central and northeastern states.

Because the terrain is so rugged, the lakes are characterized by highly irregular shorelines and numerous islands and reefs. Most have an abundance of deep, cold water. But with so much bedrock in the basin and surrounding terrain, the water tends to be low in nutrients.

The infertile water, combined with the short open-water season, means the food supply – and gamefish production – is comparatively low. Consequently, the lakes cannot tolerate heavy fishing pressure. Remote, hard-to-reach lakes produce good-sized fish, but once the lakes become popular, gamefish size declines rapidly. Canadian natural-resources agencies are attempting to solve the problem with special management, including slot limits (p. 149) and complete catch-and-release regulations.

As a result of the low productivity, there is little decaying organic matter in the depths to consume oxygen. Thus, deep-water oxygen levels are high and gamefish move vertically more than they do in fertile lakes.

Some Canadian Shield reservoirs have a "two-story" fishery. The upper story supports warmwater gamefish, such as walleyes, northern pike, muskies and smallmouth bass; the lower, coldwater species, such as lake trout, brook trout and whitefish.

Weed growth is sparse because of the deep, rocky basins and the fluctuating water. But if you can find weeds of the right kind, such as cabbage and milfoil, you'll normally find fish. The weed shortage makes the vegetation more of a fish magnet than in lakes with lush weed growth. Fish may also take cover in flooded timber.

Case Study:

Lac Seul Reservoir, Ontario, Canada

If you're not accustomed to navigating this huge man-made lake, you could easily take a wrong turn and spend the night sleeping with the bears. The lake is a maze of islands and channels, many of which look very much alike when you're on the water.

Prior to construction of a concrete gravity dam in 1930, the area that is now the reservoir included a portion of the English River and its connecting bays, as well as 12 separate lakes. The largest one, Lost Lake, covered about 14,000 acres. The dam raised the water level 16 feet, creating one gigantic body of water with a surface area of 375,000 acres.

The main purpose of the reservoir is to supply water for power generation. The water is drawn down as much as 10 feet from summer through early spring, and the lake is refilled by spring snowmelt.

The water fluctuation is enough to limit growth of submerged vegetation. Beds of Richardson's pondweed, a form of broadleaved cabbage that makes ideal gamefish cover, are scattered throughout the lake. But most of the beds are small and may be difficult to locate, particularly in high water.

You'll also find patches of flooded timber throughout the lake, especially on points and tips of islands. However, much of the timber has fallen and what's left is sparse, making poor fish cover. But if you can find timber mixed with cabbage, you'll generally find fish.

Known mainly for its outstanding walleye fishery, Lac Seul also yields plenty of northern pike and an impressive number of trophy-caliber muskies. Smallmouth bass have been introduced, and are doing well, particularly in the southeastern section of the lake. Saugers, although quite numerous, seldom grow large enough to attract much attention. Anglers fishing the deepest parts of the lake bag an occasional lake trout.

Practically all of the fishing on Lac Seul takes place from mid-May through September. There is very little ice fishing, because the currents and fluctuating water level create treacherous ice conditions.

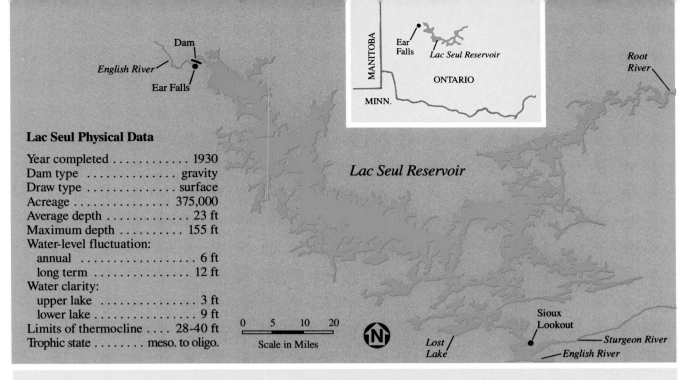

Dam
English River
Ear Falls

Root River

Lac Seul Reservoir

Lac Seul Physical Data

Year completed	1930
Dam type	gravity
Draw type	surface
Acreage	375,000
Average depth	23 ft
Maximum depth	155 ft
Water-level fluctuation:	
annual	6 ft
long term	12 ft
Water clarity:	
upper lake	3 ft
lower lake	9 ft
Limits of thermocline	28-40 ft
Trophic state	meso. to oligo.

0   5   10   20
Scale in Miles

N

Lost Lake

Sioux Lookout

Sturgeon River

English River

Information and Services

General visitor information
Travel Information Center
Box 397
Sioux Lookout, Ont., Canada POV 2TO

Biologist
Ont. Ministry of Natural Resources
Box 309
Sioux Lookout, Ont., Canada POV 2TO

Accommodations
Lost Island Lodge
R. R. 2
Emo, Ont., Canada POW 1EO

Ojibway Outfitters
Box 6 – Site 10, R. R. 1
Sioux Lookout, Ont., Canada POV 2TO

Whitewings Floating Lodges
Box 224
Ear Falls, Ont., Canada POV 1TO

Guides
Available through resorts listed

Sanctuaries have been set up on Lac Seul to preserve fishing quality

Three major rivers feed Lac Seul Reservoir – the Root, English and Sturgeon. They supply enough water to create a noticeable current, particularly in narrows near the inflows.

The upper lake, fed mainly by the Root, is relatively shallow, exceeding 40 feet in only a few spots, and is heavily bog-stained. The middle and lower sections, fed primarily by the English and Sturgeon rivers, are wider and deeper, with many areas over 80 feet, and the water has only a light bog stain.

Lac Seul has 20 full-service resorts, 12 primitive outpost camps and 3 houseboat outfitters. The outposts and houseboats provide access to the upper lake, considered the prime area for good-sized muskies, pike and walleyes.

You can launch your boat at the town of Sioux Lookout and travel to the upper end. But the distance, more than 35 miles, makes the trip impractical for a day's fishing, even if you know how to navigate through the numerous islands and reefs.

Most of the lake's resorts are located in the Ear Falls area, at the extreme lower end of the lake. This area is fished much more heavily than the upper lake, but yields good numbers of walleyes and northern pike, as well as a few muskies. The average size of the fish is less than in the upper lake, although big ones are taken regularly.

When navigating on Lac Seul, watch for the colored buoys marking major reefs and points. You must know which way the current is flowing, then keep the red buoys on your right and the green ones on your left when heading upstream. But many of the reefs are unmarked, so you'll need a detailed lake map and a depth finder that reads at high speed, preferably one with a depth alarm.

Lac Seul Habitat

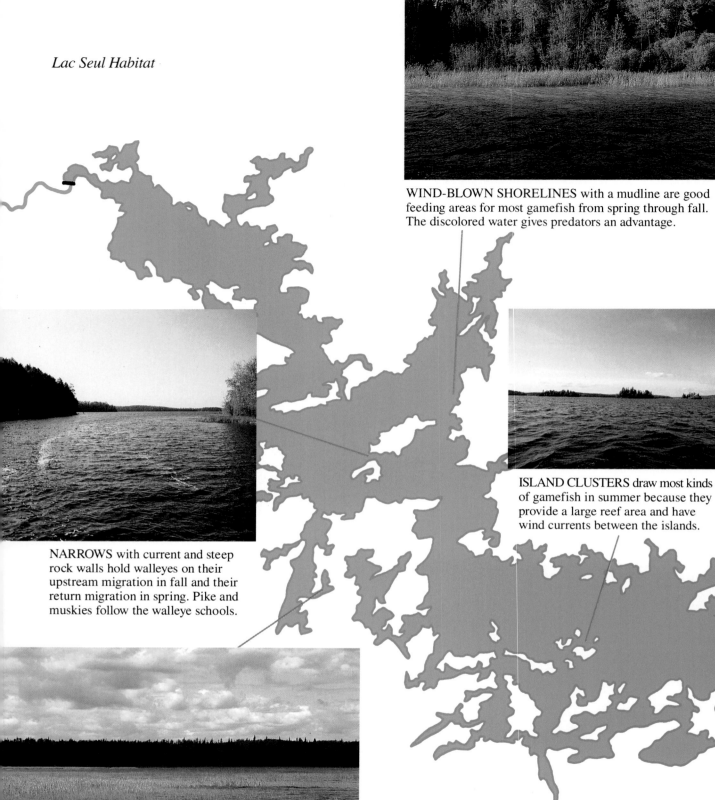

WIND-BLOWN SHORELINES with a mudline are good feeding areas for most gamefish from spring through fall. The discolored water gives predators an advantage.

ISLAND CLUSTERS draw most kinds of gamefish in summer because they provide a large reef area and have wind currents between the islands.

NARROWS with current and steep rock walls hold walleyes on their upstream migration in fall and their return migration in spring. Pike and muskies follow the walleye schools.

SHALLOW BAYS, particularly those fed by small streams, make ideal spawning areas for pike and muskies, and hold small pike into the summer.

ROCKY REEFS adjacent to deep water hold smallmouths from spring through fall; walleyes, muskies and pike, in summer and fall.

RIVERS flowing into the lake begin drawing walleyes in fall, although the fish won't spawn until spring. Pike and muskies follow the walleyes on their upstream migration.

GRASSY ISLANDS with cabbage beds along the fringes make good summertime habitat for pike, muskies and smallmouth bass.

TIMBERED POINTS with cabbage are excellent summertime spots for muskies, pike, walleyes and smallmouths. They hold few fish after the weeds die.

SADDLES with timber and cabbage make prime summertime pike and muskie hangouts. Rocky saddles are better for smallmouth bass and walleyes.

143

Lac Seul Reservoir:

Muskie

When you come to Lac Seul, don't forget your camera. The lake's burgeoning reputation for giant muskies has led to establishment of special regulations intended to preserve the reservoir's world-class muskie fishery for years to come: all muskies caught must be returned to the water immediately.

Although you can find muskies anywhere in Lac Seul, the largest concentration – and the most big fish – are in the upper one-third of the lake. The water in the upper reaches is much shallower, warmer and weedier, making for better muskie habitat.

Currently, the muskie season opens on the third Saturday in June. By then, only a few fish remain in the back ends of the bays where they spawned. Most of them have moved toward islands or major points near the mouths of the bays.

By mid-July, muskies have zeroed in on beds of newly emerged cabbage. Wherever you find cabbage beds adjacent to water at least 15 feet deep, you have a good chance of catching a muskie.

Cabbage beds in the backs of shallow bays, or beds with no easy access to deep water, hold lots of pike but seldom a muskie.

When the cabbage begins to turn brown, usually in late August, muskies become more rock-oriented. Look for them on points and reefs, preferably those with big boulders, that drop sharply into water at least 30 feet deep. These areas continue to produce until late fall.

RIGHT WAY. Cradle the fish with one hand beneath the head and the other just behind the belly. Be sure there is no lure in the fish's mouth; if it should flop, you could be seriously injured. Return the fish to the water within a few seconds.

Beginning in September, muskies also hold in narrows between large open-water areas or leading into a bay. There, they find large numbers of walleyes that are moving toward the rivers where they will spawn in spring.

Casting big lures and setting the hook in a muskie's bony mouth require stout tackle. A 6½- or 7-foot, heavy-power, fast-action baitcasting rod and a high-speed reel spooled with 30- to 50-pound Dacron line work well for most types of muskie fishing.

A 6-foot, heavy-power rod would be a better choice for casting jerkbaits or for trolling. Always use a top-quality, heavy-wire leader (p. 153).

Lac Seul muskie anglers use a wide variety of techniques, depending on the type of habitat, time of day and weather. The following pages show you the best muskie tactics for the conditions you're most likely to encounter.

WRONG WAY. Do not lift the fish by the gills. While this technique may be acceptable for smaller fish, the sheer weight of a big fish could cause the gill arch to tear, especially if the fish starts to thrash. And the razor-sharp gill rakers could cut your hand.

Fishing the Cabbage

Cabbage beds are prime muskie habitat from the beginning of the season through late summer, when the weeds start to die off. They're best early and late in the day, or when the wind is blowing into them.

In early season, look for cabbage beds from 3 to 5 feet deep in shallow bays. In summer, 6- to 8-foot beds in the main lake are more productive. Some of the best cabbage beds are surprisingly small.

Fishing the Rocks

Rocky points and humps in the main lake become the preferred muskie habitat once the cabbage dies off. They continue to produce through fall. The best rocky structure is near water at least 30 feet deep.

You'll also find some muskies on rocky points just outside the spawning bays in early season, usually at depths of 15 feet or less.

On cloudy or windy days, fish tight to the structure with jerkbaits or bucktails. On calm, sunny days, work crankbaits down the breaks.

Trolling

Trolling is particularly effective in late fall, when big muskies move into narrows with moving water to feed on the walleyes that congregate there.

This technique also works well on sunny days in summer and early fall, when muskies are hanging just off structure, such as points, reefs, saddles and island clusters.

When fishing is slow, trolling may be more effective than casting, because you're covering more territory and your lure is always in the water.

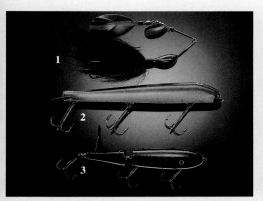

LURES include: (1) Lindy Giant Tandem Spin spinnerbait; (2) Bobbie Bait, a high-riding jerkbait; (3) Gooch's Tally Wacker, a topwater tailspin.

LOOK for patches of cane as an indicator of cabbage beds. Cabbage often grows in slightly deeper water just outside the cane.

PLUNGE a topwater beneath the surface to tempt a following muskie to strike. The fish may think its meal is getting away and grab the lure.

LURES include: (1) Suick Muskie Thriller, a diving jerkbait; (2) Bagley DB-08, a deep-diving crankbait; (3) Windel's Harasser bucktail.

RIP a crankbait to the surface by sweeping your rod high and reeling rapidly. The sudden change in speed and direction may trigger a strike.

SCREW a strip of metal under the nose of a jerkbait to prevent damaging the wood on the rocks. This adds to the life of your lure.

LURES include: (1) Bomber Long A, a deep-diving minnow plug; (2) Bucher Depth Raider, a deep-diving crankbait; (3) Believer, a trolling plug.

TROLL with wire line for better depth control. It sinks much more rapidly than mono or Dacron, so you won't have to let out as much line.

SWEEP your rod forward periodically when trolling. The erratic action may draw a strike from a muskie that is following the lure.

Big crankbaits produce big walleyes

Lac Seul Reservoir:
Walleye

Lac Seul is one of the rare lakes that produces good-sized walleyes and lots of them. When conditions are right, you'll catch dozens of 1- to 2-pounders in a day, with a fair shot at a fish from 8 to 12. To protect this outstanding walleye fishery, the Ontario Ministry of Natural Resources has established a *slot limit*, making it mandatory to release all walleyes within a given length range, currently 18 to 21 inches (about 2 to 3 pounds).

You can only keep walleyes that are outside the "slot"

With such an abundance of walleyes, fishing techniques and locational patterns need not be as precise as in a typical walleye lake. Anglers casting magnum lures for muskies in midsummer often catch walleyes in depths of 5 feet or less, while fishermen targeting walleyes are catching them on live bait in depths of 25 feet or more.

More important than the exact depth or presentation is finding the area of the lake that is holding walleyes at a given time of year. Because of the powerful riverine influence, walleyes in Lac Seul are highly migratory.

You'll catch the highest percentage of big walleyes in fall, from the middle of September to freeze-up, when the fish begin migrating toward the rivers where they will spawn in spring. Look for large walleye schools at depths of 10 to 25 feet in narrows, along deep reefs and on current-brushed points just below the mouths of spawning streams. Some of the areas of heaviest fall walleye concentration, however, are closed to fishing in fall and remain closed until well after the fish have finished spawning in spring. Be alert for signs posting these sanctuaries.

When you locate tightly schooled walleyes, try casting to them with a $1/8$- to $1/4$-ounce jig tipped with a 3- to 5-inch minnow. A $5\frac{1}{2}$-foot, medium-power, fast-action spinning outfit with 6- to 8-pound mono is ideal for jig fishing.

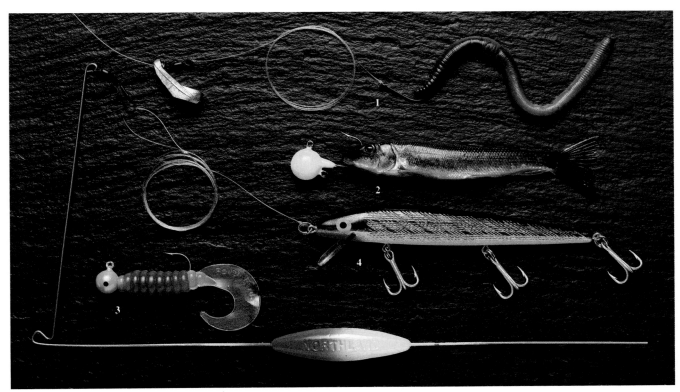

LURES for walleyes include: (1) slip-sinker rig with night-crawler, (2) Northland Fireball Jig tipped with a minnow, (3) Berkley Power Grub on jig, (4) Northland Rock-Runner bottom-bouncer rig with Rebel Minnow Floater.

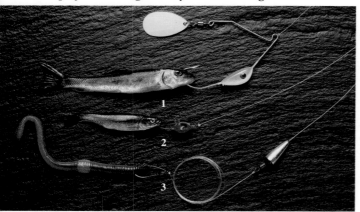

LURES AND BAITS for fishing in cabbage include: (1) Gopher Live-Bait Spin; (2) John Myhre Weedless Jig; (3) slip-sinker rig with bullet weight and weedless hook, baited with a nightcrawler.

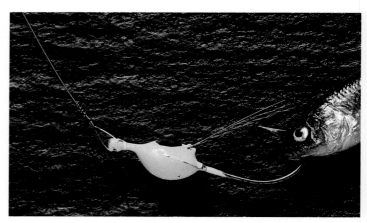

ADD a 4- to 6-inch wire leader to prevent pike bite-offs. Haywire-twist the lure to one end of a piece of 20-pound, single-strand wire; a barrel swivel to the other end. The leader will not reduce the lure's effectiveness.

Walleye season closes lakewide in mid-April, to protect the spawners. Except in the sanctuaries, it opens again on the third Saturday in May. By then, the fish are either in the late stages of spawning, or have just finished, so they're still concentrated near their spawning grounds. Fish for them much the same way you would in fall.

The walleyes turn on around mid-June, when they've recovered from the stress of spawning and are working their way back toward their summer haunts. Narrows are key locations at this time, because all fish moving downstream must funnel through them. Jig fishing at depths of 10 to 25 feet is still the most productive technique.

Walleyes settle into their summertime pattern by early July. You'll find most of the fish in the main lake, usually on reefs or on points with extended lips. The primary depth range in summer is 15 to 30 feet, but it's not unusual to catch some fish in cabbage beds, at depths of 5 to 8 feet (above).

The secret to finding walleyes is locating hard-bottomed structure. Much of the bottom in Lac Seul is covered with a thick layer of sediment – not what walleyes prefer. With a good graph, however, you can quickly identify the right bottom type, as the photo at left shows.

A hard bottom looks solid; a soft bottom, fuzzy

Backtrolling with an ordinary ¼- to ⅜-ounce slip-sinker rig, baited with a leech, nightcrawler or minnow, accounts for a high percentage of walleyes in summer. A 6½-foot, medium-power, soft-tipped spinning outfit with 6-pound mono works well for live-bait fishing.

The majority of Lac Seul's walleye structure, though firm, is not as rocky and snaggy as in most natural Canadian Shield lakes, so there's usually no need for special snag-resistant rigs or heavy line. If you're having problems with snags, however, try a bottom-bouncer rig (p. 149) or a dropper rig (p. 155).

Jig fishing is just as effective in summer as in spring and fall. Cast or slow-troll with a ⅛- to ¼-ounce jig tipped with a small minnow or a 3-inch soft-plastic curlytail.

Another productive summer and fall technique, particularly for good-sized walleyes, is trolling with 5- to 7-inch floating minnow plugs. Toss out enough markers so you can easily follow the breakline, attach the plug to a bottom-bouncer or three-way swivel rig with a 2-ounce weight, then troll parallel to the break. And don't be surprised if you hook a big pike or muskie while you're at it.

Lac Seul walleyes often feed from dawn until dusk, with no midday lull. But they may go deeper as the sun rises higher. In summer, for instance, you'll often catch them at 15 feet in early morning, but they may drop to 30 feet in mid-afternoon. The bite slows considerably after the sun goes down.

Because of the dark water in Lac Seul, cloud cover and wind have less effect on walleye activity than in a clearer lake, although the fish move a little shallower on windy days.

LOOK for cabbage beds in sheltered areas, such as the lee of an island or point, or a protected bay. Cabbage seldom grows along exposed shorelines or in other areas subjected to the full force of the wind.

CAST into pockets along the fringes of cabbage beds. If the lure hangs up, a sharp jerk will usually free it. If you try to retrieve through dense cabbage, bits of leaves will continually foul your lure.

Tips for Finding Walleyes

CURRENT ZONES in major narrows or necked-down channels between islands draw walleyes because of the abundance of baitfish in these areas.

CHANNEL MARKERS may double as walleye markers because they're often placed on rocky reefs and points used by walleyes in the summer.

SANDY POINTS with long extensions, particularly those in the main lake, are excellent summertime walleye spots.

The walleyes normally hang just off the tip of the point, at depths of 15 to 25 feet.

It's not unusual for a big pike to grab a hooked walleye and refuse to let go

Lac Seul Reservoir:

Northern Pike

The maze of weedy bays projecting off the main body of Lac Seul is paradise for northern pike. Although many local fishermen hold pike in low esteem, referring to them as "jacks," they're a favorite of visiting anglers.

Pike run 4 to 12 pounds in Lac Seul, but there's a good chance of connecting with some that are bigger – much bigger. The lake produces fish in the 25- to 30-pound class each year.

You'll find pike everywhere you find muskies, and in many other places as well. As a rule, pike prefer denser weeds, so they're more likely to be in the back ends of bays or in shallow weed clumps along the shoreline.

The bays where pike spawn are shallower and weedier than those used by spawning muskies. Pike generally complete spawning by early May, but some fish stay in the spawning bays through June. Casting with spoons, minnow plugs and small jerkbaits accounts for most early-season pike.

Because there's always a chance of hooking a giant pike, many Lac Seul pike anglers use muskie tackle (p. 147). But if the big lures aren't working, you may want to scale your tackle down a bit.

152

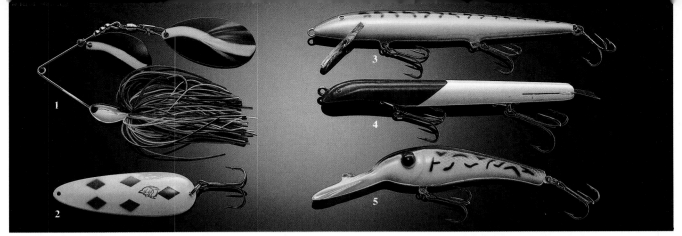

LURES for pike include: (1) Lindy Big Fin, a tandem-blade spinnerbait; (2) Eppinger Dardevle; (3) Original Floating Rapala minnow plug; (4) Suick Pike Thriller, a diving jerkbait; (5) Lindy Shadling, a medium-running crankbait.

Tips for Lac Seul Pike

FLATTEN the barbs on your hooks for easy removal. This way, you can release the fish unharmed.

STEER your lure through slots in the cabbage (dotted line) to reduce the chances of fouling.

WEDGE a sharpened stick in a pike's mouth if you don't have a spring-type jaw spreader.

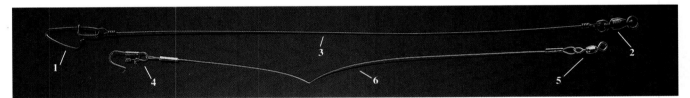

GOOD VS. BAD LEADERS. A good leader for pike and muskie fishing (top) has a (1) strong cross-lock snap, a (2) ball-bearing swivel and (3) single-strand wire of at least 40-pound test. A poor leader (bottom) has a (4) flimsy snap; (5) cheap swivel and (6) plastic-coated braided wire, which kinks easily and can't be straightened.

As the water warms, pike gradually move to the outer reaches of the spawning bays or to deeper bays. By mid-July, you'll find them in the same cabbage beds used by muskies, and on shallow, rocky points and reefs in the main lake.

Early to midsummer techniques for pike are much the same as for muskies (p. 146), but once the surface temperature reaches 70°F, big pike retreat to deeper, cooler water. Walleye anglers fishing main-lake reefs at depths of 20 to 30 feet are often surprised when they hook into a huge pike.

Trolling with big crankbaits and minnow plugs is the most productive late summer technique. Use a deep diver and a heavy baitcasting outfit spooled with 20- to 30-pound mono. With a shallow-running plug,

you'll need a 2- to 3-ounce bottom bouncer or three-way-swivel rig, or 40- to 50-pound wire line, to get the lure to the proper depth.

As the weather cools and submerged weeds die, pike move to water from 15 to 25 feet deep. Look for them along rocky reefs or in the narrows, either in deep holes or along steep rock walls. Often, they're near large schools of walleyes. Use the same trolling tactics as you would in late summer.

Pike bite best when skies are overcast. You can catch them when the weather is calm and sunny, but they're often buried in dense weeds. Cold fronts may slow the action a little, but they have less effect on pike than on most other fish species. You'll seldom catch a pike after dark.

Lac Seul Reservoir:
Smallmouth Bass

Introduced in the 1930s, small-mouth bass have adapted well to Lac Seul. The fish were stocked in the southeastern part of the lake, so that area was colonized first, but they're now appearing throughout the lake.

Lac Seul's shallow, rocky reefs teem with crayfish, the small-mouth's preferred food, so it's no wonder the introduction was a success. If you see lots of crayfish in the shallows on a point or reef, chances are the structure will hold smallmouths.

With such an abundance of food, smallmouths run good-sized. They average almost 2 pounds, and there's a reasonable chance for fish weighing 5 pounds or more.

Although the bass season is open year-round, few smallmouths are caught until mid-June, when they congregate to spawn in shallow, hard-bottom bays, on shallow reefs and along islands. If you cruise the shoreline on a calm day, you can spot their nests, and sometimes the fish. A male sweeps the gravel or rubble with his tail, leaving a clean, light-colored circle from 1 to 2 feet in diameter in 3 to 10 feet of water.

When you find a nesting area, work it thoroughly with a ⅛-ounce cur-lytail jig or a topwater, such as a small propbait. Another excellent method is working a small floating minnow plug on the surface with a twitch-and-pause retrieve. All of these techniques can be done with a 5½- to 6-foot, medium-light spinning outfit and 6- to 8-pound monofilament.

Males guard the nests for about two weeks after spawning, but females go deeper and refuse to bite. They begin showing up, along with the males, on main-lake reefs and points in mid-July. You'll find most of the fish at depths of 4 to 12 feet.

Curlytail jigs, jig-and-leech combinations and crayfish-pattern crankbaits are the mainstay of summertime smallmouth anglers. Small topwaters also work well on calm mornings and evenings.

For jigging and topwater fishing, use the same medium-light spinning gear as in spring; for crankbaiting, a 6-foot, medium-power baitcasting outfit with 8- to 10-pound monofilament.

Smallmouths, like most other Lac Seul gamefish, spend at least some of their time in cabbage, especially when the vegetation is green and lush. When fishing the cabbage, use the jigging technique recommended for walleyes (p. 150-151), including the short wire leader to prevent pike bite-offs.

Fall is prime time for big smallmouths. Beginning in late August, you'll find them along steep shorelines, reefs and points, usually at depths of 15 to 35 feet. Back-troll these areas with a slip-sinker rig and live bait, particularly big minnows (right).

Smallmouths feed most heavily in warm, stable weather. They'll continue to bite as long as this weather pattern holds, regardless of cloud cover or wind conditions. But cold fronts push the fish off the shallow reefs into deeper water and slow their feeding.

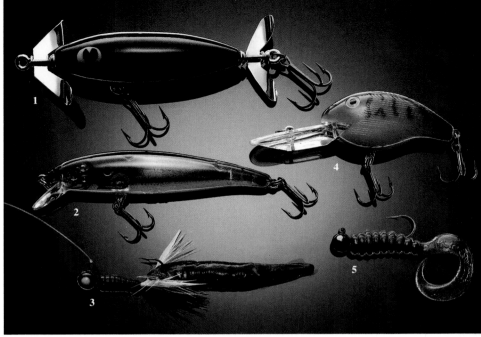

LURES for smallmouth bass include: (1) Poe's Ace in the Hole, a twin-blade propbait; (2) Bomber Long A, a floating minnow plug; (3) Lindy Fuzz-E-Grub jig, tipped with a leech; (4) Rebel Deep Wee-R, a deep-diving crankbait; (5) Mister Twister Meeny jig.

Tips for Catching Smallmouths

ROCKY POINTS with plenty of broken chunks, rather than smooth slabs, are prime smallmouth spots from early summer through fall. Long points adjacent to deep water hold the most fish.

RAPIDS have numerous boulders and eddies where smallmouths can get out of the current and ambush baitfish. The rocks also harbor crayfish. Rapids are most productive in summer and fall.

TIE a snag-resistant dropper rig as shown. The floater keeps the bait above the rocks, and if the split shot snags up, you'll lose only the shot – not the rig.

TRY 5- to 6-inch minnows to catch big smallmouths in fall. The fish prefer larger baits in late season, because young-of-the-year baitfish are larger.

Index

Cy DeCosse offers
Hunting & Fishing Products
at special subscriber discounts.
For information write:

Hunting & Fishing Products
5900 Green Oak Drive
Minnetonka, MN 55343